Urban Renewal
Municipal Revitalization

The Case of Curitiba, Brazil

Hugh Schwartz

Copyright © 2004 by
Hugh Schwartz, Ph.D.
5902 Mount Eagle Drive
#1004
Alexandria, VA 22303-2519
(703) 317-8243

Printed in the United States of America
2nd printing 2006

ISBN 0-914927-43-4

Library of Congress Control Number: 2004091833

Contents

Introduction

Brazilian industrialization increased rapidly in the 1930s and 1940s, primarily in response to balance of payments difficulties. Significant investment in new capacity was undertaken only during a few of those years, though mainly in the latter half of the 1930s. That changed in the 1950s. There was a shift from emphasis on industrialization for essentially defensive purposes to an acceleration of industrialization as a means of modernizing the economy and stimulating more rapid economic growth. A wide range of foreign trade and exchange rate mechanisms were used to attract foreign investment aimed at substituting for imports, especially consumer goods and automobiles at first. By 1962, policy sought to move beyond mere import-substituting-industrialization to help expedite the transfer of resources from abroad (and later, also to promote manufacturing exports). After the political crisis of the early-mid 1960s and the economic slowdown to which it contributed, growth resumed at an extraordinary pace. From 1968-74, Brazil's GDP rose at an annual average of more than 11 percent—nearly 13 percent for the industrial sector. However, in 1973-74, OPEC, the international cartel, raised oil prices dramatically, a major shock for an economy so dependent on imports of petroleum. The country decided to follow a policy of growing its way out of the petroleum crisis. Petrodollars were borrowed from abroad and GDP expanded at an average of about 7 percent a year in the mid-late 1970s until the effects of the 1979 increases in petroleum prices set in. The rate of growth was lower than in the preceding boom years, and the new industrialization more dependent on government investment.

The urban reawakening of Curitiba outlined in this book, dependent to a considerable extent on private industrial response to public initiatives, took place during this period of lesser growth in Brazilian GDP and, in the beginning at least, greater emphasis on government's direct involvement in industry (particularly in heavy industry). Pollution was an increasingly notable byproduct of much of the new industry. While some observers viewed that with concern, the overwhelming number of those promoting development took the position that the country needed more industry, and that negative aspects of industrialization such as pollution should be dealt with only after much more industrialization was achieved. This may have been a factor in explaining why some plans for urban renewal never were acted upon—despite the pressing need to do so, as in Greater São Paulo. Another phenomenon accompanying, sometimes facilitating the new industrialization was increased inflation, and the combination of that inflation and certain policies regarding industry, tended to reduce the share of national income going to the poor below even previously low levels.

*   *   *

Southwest of São Paulo, but seemingly a world apart, lies the Brazilian City of Curitiba. Not so modernistic as Brasilia, nor so overwhelming and problem-ridden as São Paulo, Curitiba has come to symbolize a mix of public planning initiatives and private sector responses that provides an alternative, forward-looking approach to the restructuring of medium size urban centers.

Here is a city with a per capita income that catapulted from somewhat below the national average to 65 percent above it in less than a generation, a community in which park and recreation space increased dramatically even as the population more than tripled. Curitiba has received international recognition for ecological achievements and has been an innovator or a thoughtful follower in many matters affecting the less privileged in a country with one of the greatest extremes in income distribution in the world. All is hardly perfect, but clearly, what has taken place in Curitiba calls for much closer examination. Yet though urban planners, historians, political scientists and others have expressed their judgments about the Curitiba experience, this is perhaps the first effort of an economist to do so (though it is aimed primarily at urban specialists and Latin Americanists). Even Brazilian economists have yet to attempt a major evaluation of this extraordinary socioeconomic phenomenon.

During a late 1990s symposium assessing the accomplishments of urban planning in Curitiba, Jorge Wilheim, the principal author of the city's renowned Master Plan for Redevelopment, observed that his firm also submitted a plan for the urban renewal of another relatively nearby city in the same year as the recommendations for Curitiba were drawn up—an even more innovative plan, he assured the audience. Yet one does not hear of comparably important changes that followed in the then industrially more advanced community of Joinville. Those who elaborated upon and implemented the guidelines prepared for Curitiba, while professionally able men and women, might not claim much more than that for themselves, and they acknowledge that they made mistakes along the way. Several of them had worked on plans for the urban renewal of other cities in Brazil and one prominent among them, when asked what he learned from those earlier exercises, replied that primarily, he learned what *not* to do. There is no pretense that those who became involved in Curitiba's redevelopment came close to obtaining the best results possible, and indeed, they would have been hard pressed to define what optimization would have involved, given the multiplicity of objectives and the changing circumstances. Yet this group achieved what may be the most successful urban renewal of any sizable municipality in the world during the late Twentieth Century—certainly one of the very most successful.

The message for other communities is this: what took place in Curitiba was accomplished with no more than a plausible set of guidelines, a strong sense of mission, and attention to the detail of implementation. The interest of the planners in becoming involved in implementation, the establishment of a large and active new city agency dedicated to that, and a willingness of the planners to become enmeshed in day-to-day municipal politics all were crucial. Continuity in approach during the initial twelve years also was important. So, too, were commentaries about the on-going process—including criticisms that began to be taken into account once critical aspects of the city's revitalization were in place. The sometimes-derided "Marketing of Curitiba," also was important, contributing to the city's development in a manner which recent findings on the border of psychology and economics make clearer, but which those responsible for the changes seem to have sensed even as they were first being set forth by academics. What transpired did contribute to a more positive sense of identity for many of those who lived in the city.

The rate of economic growth of Curitiba since 1970 has exceeded that registered in any of the other half dozen large cities of Brazil, and has equaled or exceeded that of medium-sized communities closer to the vast Greater São Paulo market. At the same time, indices of the quality of life have risen for the majority of the inhabitants, probably more so than in any other large city in Brazil. A late 1990s United Nations study terms Curitiba the Brazilian state capital with the highest living standards and lowest number of people living in poverty. Many of the policies adopted by the city had less to do with traditional economic rationality than with teachings of the disciplines of the architects, urban planners and engineers who designed the policies and dominated Curitiba politics. The policies have reflected development visions of the individuals from those fields who emerged as the community leaders. In perhaps no other major urban renewal in the entire world have economists, lawyers and investment bankers played so secondary a role.

Whether Curitiba has begun to lose some of its momentum or not, the achievements of the last three-to-four decades compare so favorably with those of most other cities that they merit a special chapter in the history of economic growth and urban development. The experience of the city calls into question any inclination to seek even increased economic welfare by the use of traditional economic policies alone. Moreover, though a number of enterprises do not claim that improvement in the quality of life was an important consideration in their decision to make or increase investments in the Curitiba Metropolitan Area, this overview suggests that such quality of life considerations did indeed play a role in many of those decisions. The imaginative construction of public works not ordinarily conceived as economic infrastructure seems to have contributed to the relatively greater rise in income levels as well as to the improvement in the quality of life.

Curitiba's success derives primarily from three considerations, which are the underlying themes of this presentation.

First, what took place in Curitiba has had more to do with individual visions and their implementation than with the comprehensive urban planning to which it is so often attributed.

Second, that implementation has aimed at improvement, often relatively rapid improvement—rarely at optimization of any kind. The decision making has relied heavily on the use of heuristics—Rules of Thumb—and one of the keys to the success of that decision making may have been an ability to recognize important biases involved in the use of those Rules of Thumb. That recognition must have been attributable in large measure to the profound understanding that Jaime Lerner and his group of municipal leaders had of their city and its institutions.

Third, the principal contribution of Curitiba's success has not been the rejuvenation of its downtown area, the unique restructuring of its public transportation system, nor even the ability to so alter the city's economic base as such, but the way in which all these have been accomplished. While architects and urban planners praise the first of these, transportation economists the second, and the populace at large, the last of these (with their votes), few show enough concern for what is the city's true legacy—the way in which all of this has been accomplished. At this time, the key challenge to Curitiba is to better explain that legacy, the way in which the visions have been implemented and the city transformed, before the principal contributors to the process leave the scene or simply forget vital details of what was done and why.

This presentation is based on extensive written materials and on interviews with nearly a hundred individuals, a majority from the private sector, at least at the time of the interviews. It outlines the Curitiba experience and asks about its relevance beyond the city's borders. A number of communities in Brazil and abroad already turn to Curitiba for advice about one aspect or another of urban development. Consider two examples. For several years in the 1990s the Argentine Ambassador to Brazil arranged for a dozen officials from his country's cities to spend a week in Curitiba, observing the way in which the community's institutions functioned. Second, at least 18 cities in the United States have been considering modifications of their public transportation system that would incorporate some of the lessons learned from Curitiba and a dozen of those communities sent representatives to Brazil in December 2000 to observe the situation first-hand.[1] It may be too late to obtain critical information necessary to resolve several of the politically charged controversies concerning Curitiba's development, but perhaps this account will stimulate others to analyze the city's experience more fully and encourage those responsible for so much of the change to explain more of the reasoning underlying their decisions. What has taken place in Curitiba should prove of great interest to those beyond the city's borders who yearn for a rejuvenation of their own metropolitan areas.

Most of the materials I have relied upon were gathered in 1995, 1997 and 1998 while teaching in the Department of Economics of the Federal University of Paraná, first as a Fulbright Lecturer, and then as a Visiting Professor. In addition, I have benefited from materials and discussions at the World Bank and the Inter-American Development Bank (IDB) with leaders of the Curitiba experience, particularly in an IDB seminar on Curitiba in 1996 and in another on the municipal development program of the State of Paraná in 1999. The bibliography lists those with whom I held interviews of substance. Let me begin, though, by acknowledging the interviews that were particularly important, along with those who offered comments on earlier drafts of this manuscript. I have drawn on many of the interviews although it has not been possible to include some information in what follows, particularly certain information of a personal nature. While I spoke at some length with a number of key figures of the Lerner Group, I had only three brief conversations with Jaime Lerner, one following a public presentation in Curitiba and two others in Washington. Nonetheless, Governor Lerner was kind enough to read the next-to-last draft of the manuscript and offered comments, all of which are noted either in the text or the endnotes.

Although my initial interest in Curitiba was stirred by comments overheard while I lived in Uruguay in the early-to-mid 1990s, my major debts are to the Fulbright Commission and to the Department of Economics of the Federal University of Paraná. The latter first recommended that I be brought to Curitiba as a Fulbright Lecturer, and subsequently invited me back as a Visiting Professor.

Of the interviews, I want to single out one with Cassio Taniguchi, Mayor of the city, and long a leading collaborator in the urban renewal of Curitiba. Subsequently, Mayor Taniguchi gave a draft of this manuscript to Maria do Rocio Morais do Rosario Quandt of IPPUC, the Planning and Research Institute of Curitiba, for her comments. Ms. Quandt, who made the principal exposition to the group of officials from American cities in December 2000, provided extensive and very helpful observations.

Of the other interviews, I want to express my gratitude to Luis Carlos Baeta Viera, Isac Baril, Roberto Barion, Gilson Mueller Berneck, Ivo Luiz Boschetti, Oscar Fenner Boye, Helio Cadore, Antoninho Caron, Demian Castro, Carlos Ceniviva, Carlos Decker Neto, Daniel Fedato, Orly Fedato, Maria Elisa Ferraz Paciornik, Miguel Fuentes Sala, Ramón Vicente García Fernández, Lubomir Dunin Ficinski, Claus Germer, Nelson Robert Hubner, Carlos Artur Kruger Passos, Gilmar M. Lourenço, Francisco de Borja Baptista de Magalhães Filho, Paulo A. Maranhão Faria, Mariano de Matos Macedo, Ulisses Mauad, Wilhem Meiners, Carlos Morassutti, Renato Requião Munhoz da Rocha, Marcos Mueller Schlemm, João Noma, Dennison de Oliveira, Eduilton Ostroski, Roberto Paredo, Sergio Prosdócimo, Karlos Richbieter, Vilson Ronald Riles Deconto, Jose Rimi, André R. de Ruediger, Julio Salamão, Miguel Salamão, Jorge Samek, Humberto Sanches Netto, Maurilio Schmidt, Adair Springer Passos, Pedro Jose Steiner, Jorge Eduardo Supliciy Funaro, Kentaro Takahara, André Zacharow, the librarians at IPPUC and IPARDES and one or two staff members at IPPUC who might prefer not to be identified. Professor Dennison de Oliveira kindly furnished me with a draft of *Curitiba e o mito da cidade modelo* (as well as a draft of research he was initiating) and listened patiently to my comments concerning his research (which comments I also provided in writing). Professor Oliveira's work is the single most important publication on Curitiba, in my opinion, but his presentation of a few points strikes me as marred.

In addition to the comments from Governor Jaime Lerner, I am most grateful for extensive comments to an earlier version from Maria Quandt, as also noted above, to Professor Marshall Eakin of Vanderbilt University, and to the late Charles Wright, formerly of the Inter-American Development Bank, who was kind enough to make his collection of photographs available to me. My appreciation, too, for comments to Michael Berger, Ivo Luiz Boschetti, Joseph Goodman, Renato Requião Munhoz da Rocha, Lloyd Schwartz and Stephen Schwartz. I have incorporated many, but by no means all their observations.

This short volume is aimed, first, at presenting urban planners and general readers particularly concerned with improving their own urban environment with a concise overview of what took place in one of the world's most successful cases of municipal revitalization. Those in Latin American studies also should find the book of interest. For many of them, the Curitiba experience is much cited though perhaps still not adequately understood. Finally, I hope that what follows will attract economists as well—particularly urban and regional economists, transportation economists, and the rapidly expanding group of behavioral economists.

The map of the transportation network of Curitiba was provided from the archives of IPPUC by Oscar Schmeiske who also helped me obtain photographs from Curitiba's Municipal Secretariat of Social Communication. Additional photographs were obtained from the collection of Charles Wright with the assistance of Gloria and Elisson Wright. Paulo Krauss of the Jaime Lerner Institute provided notes that served as the basis for Appendix C. Appendix A is based on Appendix A in Hugh Schwartz, *Rationality Gone Awry? Decision Making Inconsistent with Economic and Financial Theory* (1998, Westport, CT and London, Praeger Publishers, paperback: 2000) and is included in this modified version with the permission of the Greenwood Publishing Group, Inc. José Ellauri designed the covers of the book.

---

[1]   See U.S. Department of Transportation [2001].

1

The Transformation of Curitiba

The Background

The southern Brazilian City of Curitiba has attracted attention from architects, urban planners and an increasing number of sources; it has even been mentioned in a novel by John Grisham and featured in a Brazilian film starring Anthony Quinn. About 250 miles southwest of São Paulo, and separated from the Atlantic port city of Paranaguá by a small mountain range, Curitiba is located approximately 3,000 feet above sea level at the onset of a plateau that extends westward for 500 miles, reaching to the spectacular Iguazu Falls on the border of Brazil, Argentina and Paraguay. In the year 2000, the city had a population of approximately 1,650,000, and the metropolitan region, nearly 2,600,000—the latter, only an eighth the size of Metropolitan São Paulo, but two-thirds as large as Metropolitan Belo Horizonte, which had replaced Rio de Janeiro in the early 1980s as the second largest industrial center in the country.

Curitiba is the capital of the State of Paraná, a political jurisdiction carved out of the Province, now the State of São Paulo in the mid-nineteenth century. The city is more than three hundred years old. In the late seventeenth and early eighteenth centuries, Curitiba's existence was related to the search for gold. This involved a limited amount of local prospecting, supplanted increasingly by the supply of mules to transport the precious mineral from Minas Gerais to the coast.[1] Sparse settlement and subsistence agriculture characterized Paraná throughout much of the rest of the eighteenth century and into the nineteenth century when other activities were initiated, notably those servicing more developed states to the north and to the south. The earlier trade of supplying pack animals received a new and stronger impulse with the major expansion of coffee cultivation in São Paulo in the mid-nineteenth industry. In addition, there was the breeding and winter grazing of cattle, which continued to be of consequence into the twentieth century.

Paraná, still one of the leading agricultural states of Brazil, was preeminently agricultural and agroindustrial until the late 1970s, and by many standards, until the beginning of the1990s, long known for Paraguay tea (yerba mate, an inexpensive green tea), lumber, woodworking, and to a lesser extent, cotton and other agroindustrial products. The cultivation and basic processing of Paraguay tea became important in the nineteenth century, and from 1890 through 1920, the green tea was the leading product of Paraná. Indeed, it was a major export of Brazil to Argentina, Chile and Uruguay until, in response to rising prices that resulted from a growing demand but only very limited increases in Brazilian and Paraguayan output, Argentina fostered domestic production of mate by offering substantial protection to local producers. With a declining export potential, Paraná's mate industry stagnated in the 1920s and declined in the 1930s and 1940s.

Dense pine forests covered the eastern part of the state and with the improvement of transportation facilities in the second half of the nineteenth century and the beginning of the twentieth, local lumber and woodworking activities took on more importance, receiving a further boost during World War I. The industry attracted investment from Great Britain and the United States (with a major portion of the profits from those investments channeled abroad and much of the rest to São Paulo), but the sawmills and furniture factories that sprung up remained in local hands, as did all phases of mate production. By the outset of the World War II, lumber, woodworking and mate were the most important economic activities in Paraná, with those who industrialized the products in more powerful economic positions than landowners, in contrast to the situation in most of the dominantly agricultural regions of Brazil. Nonetheless, the Federation of Industries of Paraná (FIEP) was then, and continued until the late 1990s, to be rather laid back and low key, more like a social organization than a typical industrial trade association, and less focused on industrial promotion than its counterpart in several other states with emerging manufacturing sectors.

Paraná first became an important coffee producer in the 1930s, and by the early 1960s, accounted for 60 percent of all Brazilian output and a third of world production. Some cafes in Paris and Buenos Aires posted plaques assuring their patrons that they served "Coffee from Paraná." In the early 1960s, a third of all income in the state was generated by the production of coffee, and between 1939 and the early 1960s, the state's share of Brazilian

GDP doubled. Although this brought new prosperity to the north of Paraná and to the State generally, Brazil had levied export taxes on coffee from the 1930s, and in the 1950s introduced multiple foreign exchange rates that effected a disguised tax on coffee exports. (This was mitigated to a degree by a price support program in the 1950s and the first half of the 1960s.) The revenues collected from the disguised taxes on coffee ended up as part of the funds used to subsidize industrialization—almost all of which was taking place beyond Curitiba and the rest of Paraná. Frosts, initially in 1953-54, and then more seriously in 1962-63, 1966, and 1975 brought Paraná's coffee boom to a close. The crop is now much less important for the state, replaced mainly by soybeans, which are internationally competitive, and wheat, corn, other beans, rice and sugar, which do not enjoy as favorable a position. The latter is also true of dairy products, the advancement of which has been largely attributable to the cooperatives that sprung up in the 1940s, and gained greater force in the 1960s and 1970s.

The production and processing of Paraguay tea and the woodworking activities were focused in the eastern part of the state, and Curitiba was long the dominant processing and commercialization center. The coffee boom shifted more of the agroindustrial activity north, to Londrina, a city established in the 1920s with strong financial and commercial ties to São Paulo. Maringá, to the west of Londrina, is currently the most important agroindustrial center in Paraná. That city, now the third largest in the state, was first founded in the 1950s. Curitiba's importance as an agroindustrial center has been declining relative to these two cities and to other smaller communities in western Paraná. All these locales owe their origin or major expansion to recent colonization. Indeed, while the population of Paraná totaled only 1.2 million in 1940, more than 2.7 million people immigrated into this then rapidly expanding agricultural frontier over the next twenty-five years, and they and their families accounted for two-thirds of the entire population of the state in 1965. This colonization, which was associated with an increase in the market orientation of Paraná's agriculture, drew primarily on the nearby States of São Paulo, Minas Gerais, Santa Catarina, and Rio Grande do Sul, and relatively less on foreign countries than the inflows of the late 19th and early 20th Centuries.

In 1950, Curitiba was a pleasant, rather tranquil community, a city of 180,000 whose activities revolved to a considerable extent around the official business of the State of Paraná and the University of Paraná, the first public university in Brazil, established in 1913. The industrial sector, smaller than in two cities in neighboring Santa Catarina, not to mention the four leading centers of the country, was still based overwhelmingly on agricultural inputs. There were a number of notable historic buildings—public offices, churches and private homes—and many simple but attractive homes constructed of timbers from the once abundant, distinctive pine forests of the state. But the city also was characterized by a shortage of electricity, telephones, and paved streets. Indeed, there were but 350 miles of paved highways in the State of Paraná (only a tenth of which had been funded by the state itself), and as late as 1960, part of the distance between Curitiba and Londrina, the second largest city in the state, remained unpaved. Only a third of the families living in Curitiba had access to sewers. And traffic was beginning to become more of a problem in the downtown area.

Curitiba today is a much different city. It has achieved national renown in little more than a generation—as a rapidly growing industrial center, but also as an attractive, prosperous, ecologically conscious and highly successful example of urban planning, a socioeconomic triumph among the larger Brazilian cities. Overall, Curitiba's reputation seems deserved, even if it is perhaps not quite one of the three most livable cities in the world, as an urban planning specialist from the University of California at Berkeley ventured a decade ago (which appreciation, the municipality then used in some of its promotional literature). Temperatures in the city often hover in the 40s, 50s, even reach freezing in winter (a serious matter, given the general lack of central heating in the city), and in one or two months of spring it sometimes rains for several hours during half to two-thirds of the days. Five rivers traverse the metropolitan area along with many small streams (there are nearly 2,000 miles of rivers and streams within the city's 270 square miles, some of which have become subterranean). The installation of concrete walls alongside a number of stretches of river (channelization) and the completion of major drainage/parkland improvements has reduced flooding, but until quite recently, it remained a problem in the southern part of the city. Few had lived there a generation before, and planners had hoped to keep the area relatively unoccupied, but more and more of those migrating to Curitiba set up residence there, legally or otherwise. (During the years 1997-2001, a major dredging, riverbed widening and drainage project substantially reduced the risk of flooding within the City of Curitiba itself, though problems remain just beyond the municipality's boundaries, due especially to illegal settlements in flood plains adjacent to rivers.) Living conditions in those areas remain precarious; Curitiba thus shares a number of the problems associated with other communities in the emerging world.

Curitiba's population increased 7% a year in the 1950s and nearly 6% annually in the 1960s and 1970s. Even in the decade of economic slow-down in the country, the 1980s, population increased at an annual average of more than 2% within the city limits and more than 5% in the outlying part of the metropolitan area. Since the mid-1960s when the city's development concerns began to be actively refocused, Curitiba's population has increased three-fold, but the amount of space dedicated to parks and publicly main-tained forests has risen from less than 30 square feet per inhabitant to more than 550 (with the increase by an even larger rate according to other mea-sures referred to later). In a city once virtually without parks aside from the attractive Passeio Público on the edge of downtown, the area of green space per inhabitant has reached three times the level recommended by the United Nations.

From 1950 through 1980, Curitiba was the fastest growing of all the medium-to-large size cities in Brazil. Even in the 1980s, its lesser rate of increase was one of the highest of the country's major cities, and in the 1990s, too, the rate of growth within the city limits as well as in the overall metropolitan area was again among the highest in Brazil. This has put ex-traordinary pressures on existing infrastructure and created continuing de-mands for major additions. As a consequence, the index of some common amenities is not as high as one might expect for a successful modern city, but even the worst of those is much better than in the 1950s and 60s. Per capita income was just below the national average in 1950, began to rise with Paraná's coffee boom, and increased to a much greater extent in the 1970s and thereafter. By the late 1990s per capita income was two-thirds higher than the mean for the country.

Much of downtown Curitiba is dedicated to the pedestrian. The city inaugurated Brazil's first major pedestrian mall in 1971, and there are now twenty blocks in the heart of the city paved with decorative tile in which vehicular traffic is restricted to delivery trucks at set hours. (See photo-graphs 3 and 6.) This area includes much of the historic district. If one seeks modern architecture, a mile away is the Brasilia-like complex of buildings that house the offices of the State Government of Paraná. Several of the city's major transportation axes are lined with high rise apartment houses, many with that flair of color and design for which Brazil has become fa-mous. High rise buildings have spread to other areas, too, indeed, with unusual features—there is even a condominium that rotates continuously (or did so when it was first constructed in the late 1990s, at any rate). Curitiba boasts a number of spectacular civic structures, some, such as the wire opera house and the Free University of the Environment, which have transformed abandoned quarries and other former eyesores into some of the most distinctive man-made visual attractions in the entire country (photographs 4 and 5).

Unlike city dwellers in other leading Brazilian communities (and most major cities in the Western Hemisphere), many *curitibanos* make a habit of congregating downtown after normal office hours. It's certainly not for the nightclubs, of which there are few, and it is not solely for theater and concerts, of which there are a growing number, including two in renovated buildings that had served much less artistic functions in the past. Special annual events include national music and theater festivals, a movie festival, the Christmas lighting display and pageants, and several seasonal fairs. Most significant, though, is the continuing activity along the now pedestrian thoroughfares, lined with coffee shops, restaurants and many other commercial establishments. Then, early most Friday evenings, many teenagers gather on the principal pedestrian mall. On Saturday morning their place is taken by pre-teenage painters, families out for a stroll, those who have come to listen to amateur musical groups near the park at one end of the mall, and others, on their way to the small food and flower fair in the Passeio Público, just past the other end of the mall.

On Sunday morning the center of attraction shifts a few blocks, to the extensive and colorful flea market in Garibaldi Square, featuring all varieties of wares, prepared foods, exhibits of local artists, and musical groups ranging from old-timers, strumming melodies of Paraná past, to itinerant groups from other Latin American nations. On Sunday afternoon, numerous residents take to the botanic garden and other city parks, several located adjacent to relatively low income areas, and more than a few, to the bicycle paths, now 105 miles long (photographs 7-11).

Lest one conclude that Curitiba is some sort of idyllic community, note that the inhabitants are not as warm and outgoing as in many other Brazilian cities. Long-established families receive new arrivals with reserve. This applies not only to blue collar workers and the unemployed from other Brazilian states, but also to professionals and others of middle class background, both foreign and domestic. As for the Poles, Germans, Ukrainians, Italians, Japanese and others who began arriving in the late nineteenth century, comments overheard suggest that their initial acceptance was about the same as immigrants from abroad in most other cities of the world. Curitiba has been changing but it has not been (or become) a homogeneous or an especially socially cohesive community. Disparaging remarks about those of different ethnic backgrounds, religions and races are as common as in most other cities of the Western Hemisphere, but this has not interfered with people working together. Whatever prejudices may exist have not prevented the formation of multi-ethnic business or political alliances. At the same time, those of competitive political or business groups sometimes include unwarranted stereotypes together with substantive criticism when speaking of opponents. Nonetheless, it should be noted that the current mayor is of Japanese ancestry, Paraná's senators are of Italian and Portuguese background, and twice Governor and three-times Mayor of Curitiba, Jaime Lerner, is Jewish of Polish background. One of his closest unofficial advisors was of German ancestry, and among his cabinet appointees was someone whose parents came from Lebanon as well as others of a wide range of ethnic backgrounds.

Although Curitiba has somewhat more automobiles in proportion to population than the other large cities of Brazil (more as of the late 1990s than even Brasilia, the city virtually built for the automobile), the public transportation system is regarded as a model (photographs 1, 2 and 12-16). Approximately three-quarters of weekday commuters use it. Moreover, the flat fare system provides a transportation subsidy for those less well-off, most of whom live towards the outskirts, to reach places of employment and to take advantage of the city's parks and other attractions.

Walking in downtown Curitiba is safer than in the other large cities of the country, even in the evening, though problems have become more common at night during the last few years, and safety is questionable in some of the outlying areas. Streets in the central area are generally clean, reflecting both the attitude of municipal administrations towards appearances, and its efforts to deal with unemployment and underemployment. Both of the latter are serious problems in the city, in part because they are serious problems nationally and in part because of the continuing migration of many relatively less educated and unskilled workers to a city that has sought relatively skill-intensive investments and has been increasingly successful in attracting them. Several efforts to alleviate the situation are noted later, but at least employment as street cleaners on a day-to-day basis is available for a number of those without better alternatives.

Unemployment during the 1990s sometimes reached 10-12% in Curitiba, and was of the order of 15% for the metropolitan region outside the city limits.[2] Curitiba initiated a number of programs to deal with the problem, but people continued to arrive more rapidly than the growth of suitable new opportunities; the rate of unemployment was among the highest of the major cities in the country until 1999-2000. In the late 1970s, when larger slum areas first began to appear, Curitiba's resettlement schemes and its program of constructing low income housing offset the worst manifestations of the problem, but from the '80s on, the continuing migrations into ever-more-marginal lands have led to sizable *favelas*, though not as bad as those in other large cities of Brazil. While more than 99 percent of the inhabitants have electricity and running water, only 75-80 percent can claim access to the city's sewer system. The lack of infrastructure is more serious in the surrounding municipalities of the metropolitan area, which now have a population two-thirds as great as Curitiba itself. The Metropolitan Curitiba Region Authority was established in 1973, but, until recently, political bickering between city and state governments of different party affiliations often thwarted cooperative efforts. Fortunately, there is now greater regional consciousness and coordination.

A note, which though positive for Curitiba, is disconcerting for the country—an indication of how the quality of life in the most comfortable areas of Curitiba compares with that of similar neighborhoods in São Paulo. More than a hundred, perhaps as many as several hundred São Paulo business people have chosen to reside with their families in Curitiba and to commute two-three times a week between the two cities. Given the travel time and expense involved, this is about as inconvenient as managing a plant on Route 128 outside Boston and traveling to a home in the suburbs of New York.

The Response to Paraná's Climatic Adversity

As suddenly as Paraná burst on the international scene as a major producer of coffee, its descent was even more dramatic.[3] The replacement of labor-intensive coffee cultivation with more capital- and land-intensive crops such as soybeans, wheat and corn, led to an extraordinary transformation of the State. In the late 1960s and the 1970s, nearly a third of the population was obliged to abandon farms and small towns. Paraná, which had attracted more colonists than any other Brazilian state after 1940, became an exporter of people, and on a massive scale. Some continued in agriculture in the State of São Paulo, in Matto Grosso and even in the new western frontier, Rondónia. Half of those who left the rural areas remained in Paraná, however, moving to the cities, especially to metropolitan Curitiba. In the two decades between 1960 and 1980, the urban population of the state rose from less than 35 to more than 75 percent.

How then, did Paraná and Curitiba respond?

For most people abroad who are more or less aware of the changes in Curitiba, the name of Jaime Lerner comes immediately to mind. Perhaps that is as it should be but the process of change really began with Ney Braga.

Ney Braga was born in Lapa, a small, traditional city south of Curitiba, attended a military academy and entered the army. Assigned to Curitiba early in his career, and later rotated back there, he eventually was named Chief of Police and subsequently decided to leave the military for a political career. Elected Mayor of Curitiba for the period 1954-58, he addressed himself to a number of emerging concerns, among them the restructuring of public transportation, proposals for flood control, and the creation of an urban planning department. Braga became increasingly skeptical of the adequacy of the existing plan for urban development prepared only a decade before. The activities of his administration were noteworthy enough for the Brazilian Institute of Municipal Administration to include Curitiba on its 1957 list of the ten Brazilian cities in which greatest progress had been made. When Braga decided to run for Governor in 1959-60, he drew upon studies for the development and reorientation of economic activity in Paraná that had been prepared by an agency of the previous state administration, but which were being ignored both by outgoing officials and the other candidates for the chief administrative position in the state.

As Governor from 1961-65, Braga reorganized the state's existing development agency into CODEPAR, the Development Company of Paraná. He had independent consultants work with his own advisors to prepare a Plan for the Development of Paraná (this, several years before a similar plan was prepared in Minas Gerais). Efforts were made to get more farmers to plant crops other than coffee, which had become dominant in the modern agriculture of the northern part of the State. *The most important thrust, though, was a two-pronged effort, first to strengthen Paraná's limited economic infrastructure, and then to foster more industrial activity.* CODEPAR was the first major development entity in Brazil, preceding the Northeast's better-known SUDENE by several months. Its activities were financed in large measure by an Economic Development Fund (FDE) that drew resources from taxes at first, and afterwards, primarily from compulsory loans on transactions. FDE resources were channeled to CODEPAR, which became the Development Bank of Paraná (BADEP) in 1968.

Between 1961 and 1966, most CODEPAR/ BADEP financing went to infrastructure, but by the end of the 1960s and beginning of the 1970s, industry began to receive more attention. Overall, approximately two-fifths of the financing went to increase electric power generation, and another two-fifths to other public sector infrastructure, particularly highway construction, but also to activities such as communications and sanitation. The remainder was disbursed in the form of heavily subsidized loans to enterprises (loans with interest rates below the rate of inflation). The loans were used to promote cooperatives and individual agroindustries (two-thirds of Paraná's agricultural exports had left the state in unprocessed form in 1960), but also a wide array of small producers, this in an effort to substitute for products formerly "imported" from São Paulo and other states. (The terminology reflects the influence of the Economic Commission for Latin America and ILPES, with their center/periphery analysis of economic relationships.) At first, the favored industries were foodstuffs, woodworking and textiles, but by the early 1970s, the list included tobacco, chemicals and metalworking, and by the last half of that decade, electrical, communications and transport equipment. CODEPAR and BADEP financed a fifth of fixed investment in the state during their initial years, years of economic slowdown nationally, and by the last half of the decade of the 60s, the proportion had risen to just over a third, even as the national economy was booming. Despite Paraná's history of local ownership of industry, there was little effort to follow in the footsteps of the State of Santa Catarina to the south, and foster industries that would aim at a larger, even national market. The reason appears to be that, with a few notable exceptions mentioned later, aggressive entrepreneurs seemed to be lacking in Paraná. Nonetheless, loans using FDE funds discriminated against foreign enterprises, at least initially, and there was no attempt to attract firms from São Paulo until 1967-68. What was done in Paraná has much in common with what took place in Minas Gerais, where state development institutions were even more important in financing investment in the capital city and the state, and gave particular attention to electric power and transportation infrastructure.[4]

From the outset, the administration of Ney Braga sought to strengthen Paraná's economic infrastructure, without which Curitiba's industrialization in the 1970s would not have been possible. In 1960, the availability of electric power in Paraná, even in Curitiba, was far below the average for major population centers in Brazil but it increased three-fold during the decade. In addition, when, in the mid-1960s, the Mayor of Curitiba asked CODEPAR to finance the lengthening of a major traffic artery in the city, Karlos Richbieter, then head of the Projects Department of the agency, encouraged him to present a broader proposal for municipal redevelopment— which became the famous *Plano Diretor* or "Master Plan" for the development of the city. In suggesting that, Richbieter may have been recalling the interests that Braga himself had shown when he had been mayor. He also may have been reflecting in part, the education on urban affairs that he was receiving from his wife, Franchette, an engineer who headed up the municipal planning agency that Braga had established. Five years later, Braga persuaded the governor in the then military government to designate Jaime Lerner as mayor. Afterwards, in 1979, during his second period as Governor, Braga named Lerner to head Curitiba's Administration once again. Thus, Braga greatly strengthened the infrastructure essential for the major change in Curitiba and twice took actions to assure that the person designated to run the city was a prominent technician dedicated to change.

Regional Forces Contributing to Curitiba's Recent Growth

National and regional as well as local factors have of course contributed to the growth of Curitiba. Inasmuch as the city's rise in per capita income after 1970 so exceeded that of the country as a whole, and Curitiba's fame as a progressive modern city is associated primarily with the years following the "Brazilian Miracle" of 1968-73, it is important to inquire about the role of regional economic forces. Indeed, some economists attribute Curitiba's growth principally to its relative proximity to the São Paulo market, yet separation from the latter's increasingly unfavorable living conditions—cosmopolitan but plagued by traffic congestion, the grayness of the skies due to industrial and automotive pollution, the physical deterioration of downtown's former center, the high cost of almost everything, the combative nature of labor relations, the on-going charges and apparent reality of political corruption, the sizeable number of homeless children, the seriousness of crime (and the ferocity of police and private militia response to it), the walled, not merely gated communities of the rich, and so forth.

Regional factors certainly were important, but others appear to have figured at least as much. Some communities closer to São Paulo than Curitiba also had opportunities, and while they, too, expanded, most did not grow as much or undergo as positive a socioeconomic transformation. Nor did sizable new cities spring up in this region as occurred elsewhere in Brazil—even in western Paraná, where Maringá attained a population of 250,000 in only fifty years.

More will be indicated in a later chapter concerning the forces contributing to Curitiba's growth, but consider, first, those factors mentioned by producers in explaining why they descended upon this relative backwater during the 1970s when Curitiba was first established as an industrial center to be reckoned with.

A Study of the Decision Making Factors for Locating Industries in the Metropolitan Region of Curitiba was released in 1980.[5] It was based on a survey of enterprises in three areas of Metropolitan Curitiba, but emphasized the new Industrial City (CIC) rather than the older industrial area of the city or the bordering municipalities. The newly established enterprises cited twenty-nine overlapping reasons for locating their plants in CIC, most notably: the support of local government (mentioned by 41 percent of the enterprises); good infrastructure (16 percent of the enterprises); the geographic position of Paraná in relation to the country's principal markets (14 percent); and the low cost of land (13 percent).

The support of local government included fiscal incentives, financing concessions (including equity participation arrangements similar to those adopted in Minas Gerais), energetic local support in gaining access to federal incentive mechanisms, and extensive publicity about urban planning in Curitiba. The fiscal and financial concessions varied somewhat from enterprise to enterprise, with the full terms generally kept secret (to facilitate subsequent negotiations by local authorities with prospective investors, it was maintained).

The second factor, good infrastructure, also reflected the intervention of government, both that of the city and the state. The City of Curitiba had used the right of eminent domain to purchase the land used for CIC (a tenth of the entire city) and had constructed basic services in a setting with more open green space than in perhaps any other industrial park in the world. The highways and electric generating capacity constructed by the State of Paraná in the 1960s and 70s certainly contributed to the economic justification for the location of economic activity in the state, though in the 1960s, some of that infrastructure expansion had been undertaken largely for political considerations (to impede separatist sentiment within the state) and to accommodate economic aspirations that had more to do with separation from, rather than integration with São Paulo. The fourth factor mentioned by the enterprises, the low cost of land (recently drained and given added highway access), was a key component of the CIC incentive package, and thus was also attributable to actions of local government.

All categories of industries cited the role of government support as the leading determinant for their location in the CIC. This was as true for non-durable consumer goods industries as for capital goods, intermediate goods and consumer durables. It was mentioned as the principal reason for location in Metropolitan Curitiba for enterprises from Paraná, for those from other areas in Brazil and those from abroad. For 24 of the 41 CIC enterprises interviewed, the support of local government was mentioned as the key factor, and that figure would be still higher if account were taken of the role of government in developing electric power and other infrastructure and in subsidizing the price of land. The ranking of relative proximity to São Paulo as only the third most important factor was not to deny that it was generally a precondition for locating a new plant at some destination within a certain perimeter of São Paulo, but proximity did not explain why Curitiba was chosen in preference to other locations as close or closer to the major consumer market of São Paulo-Rio-Belo Horizonte.

Interviews with local organizations such as the municipal Urbanization Company of Curitiba and the state's official development bank, as well as with individuals connected to other development institutions echoed the importance attributed by businessmen to the four factors they mentioned in the report just referred to. While it may no longer be possible to ascertain whether Curitiba's financial incentives were greater than those offered by other communities, in some cases they probably were perceived as larger. The Association of Businessmen of the Industrial City cited half a dozen factors responsible for inducing the location of firms in CIC without attempting to assess their relative importance. Those enumerated were: the strategic geographic location of Curitiba; the infrastructure of CIC; the "optimal" urban planning of Curitiba; the existence of good technical schools and universities (not yet present in some rival communities); lack of the kind of industrial concentration problems found in São Paulo; and the highly favorable living conditions offered for families by Curitiba. Even at that early stage, the role of favorable living conditions was mentioned, though, perhaps more in terms of what was hoped would emerge rather than what actually prevailed. As noted in a subsequent chapter, the enterprises interviewed in 1997 and 1998 that had established plants in CIC in the 1970s, maintained that their locational decisions at the earlier date had not been influenced by quality of life considerations, and it is not clear that Curitiba was yet such an attractive place to live in the first half of that decade.

As Curitiba industrialized further, the increased economic externalities of the area contributed to, and indeed, became a more important part of the explanation for the city's further expansion, but even those increasing regional forces were not always the result of economic factors alone.

The second set of analyses, *Studies for a Policy of Industrial Development of Paraná*, was made public in three separate reports during 1981.[6] The first dealt with industrial deconcentration and the perspectives for Paraná, the second with the geographic distribution of industry in the state, and the third with the state's mechanisms for promoting industry.

The first report outlined the growing disadvantages of production in Greater São Paulo and the competitive draw of Belo Horizonte, the southern part of the State of Minas Gerais and the interior of the State of São Paulo. It concluded that the best possibilities for Paraná were to try to compete with the interior of the State of São Paulo, whose strength rested primarily in the ease of access to the São Paulo market, and for whom the availability of suppliers and the proximity of buyers were not the most important considerations. Supporting this was a report prepared by the State of São Paulo, based on a survey of 51 enterprises that had moved from their original location in Greater São Paulo to another location within the state. Only five of those firms had considered moving to Paraná (compared to 21 that had considered relocating to Minas Gerais), and all five cited as negative factors, what they characterized as Paraná's limitations in the supply of raw materials and components. The Paraná report also referred to another analysis of 29 firms that opened plants in the Industrial City of Curitiba. The results vary somewhat from those cited above (perhaps reflecting the way in which questions were framed). Of the 29 enterprises, 24 came directly from foreign countries and 5 relocated from other states in Brazil or established new production in Curitiba. The reason most cited for the move to Curitiba was proximity to the consumer market. The political and financial support by the State government was listed next in importance, followed by proximity to suppliers. Of the group, 20 indicated that they considered alternative sites, 18 in the State of São Paulo (of which 8 specified the interior of the State), 10 in Minas Gerais, 7 in Rio Grande do Sul, 6 in Rio de Janeiro, 3 in Santa Catarina, and 3 in other locations. Of those that had also considered Minas and Rio Grande do Sul, the reason most cited for preferring Curitiba was the lesser distance from the leading market, but among the firms that considered more distant Rio Grande do Sul, almost as many also cited other factors. Of the firms that had considered locating in Minas Gerais, Rio de Janeiro and the interior of the State of São Paulo, but had decided on Curitiba, the greater support of the Government of Paraná was among the considerations most mentioned. For those firms that chose Curitiba over Greater São Paulo, the heavy industrialization of the latter was most mentioned, along with the high cost of manpower, with much less note of the greater financial support of Paraná or the lower cost of land in Curitiba. Another study was cited that assigned importance of local financial support in explaining the selection of Curitiba, though the report maintained that Minas Gerais offered comparable support.[7]

The report on the geographic distribution of industry within Paraná, contains a section entitled "The Power of Attraction of Curitiba," based on a survey of 64 enterprises established in the capital and 17 nearby. For 32 firms originating from Paraná, 21 of the 29 responses cited family and community ties as their reason for locating in Curitiba. The 23 firms from abroad specified more than two dozen reasons, 11 of which dealt with the availability and cost of labor, 7 access to ports, highways and geographic location, and 4 the low cost of labor. Similar were the responses from the companies relocating from Greater São Paulo, with the lower cost of manpower receiving greater importance. Of the 64 firms, nearly all indicated that they anticipated that any expansion in Paraná would take place in the Curitiba Metropolitan Area. Data were provided revealing that the new industries had accounted for a substantial increase in the number of intra- and interindustry transactions in the State, suggesting the increased capacity of the new firms and the previously existing enterprises to function as suppliers of industrial inputs.

The third report deals with the instruments of several Brazilian states that were used to support industry. The section on Paraná deals mainly with the FDE, the Fund for Economic Development, which was initiated in 1962 and continued to be of moderate importance in providing resources for BADEP, the development bank of the State through 1974. BNDES, the national development bank was by far the largest source in 1969 and 1972 and became the dominant source of BADEP funds until the latter's termination in the mid-1980s. But BNDES financed similar state and regional institutions throughout Brazil.

What does all of this suggest? To begin with, it confirms that much of the new, rapid growth of industry beyond São Paulo was stimulated by the adversities that had begun to plague that city. That's hardly news. In addition, it indicates that economic forces played an important role in determining the locales that benefited from the shifts in industrial activity. Also not very surprising. Moreover, the reports indicate that local support (primarily, but not solely in terms of financial considerations) was important in explaining the relocation of industry, and, given the differential changes in the per capita income of the various Brazilian cities that took place after 1970, the implication is that the subsidization granted by Curitiba (essentially the same as that extended by several other large cities) yielded highly favorable returns to the city.

Finally, while the analyses make little mention of quality of life as a factor influencing private investment in Curitiba during the city's first major thrust of industrialization, consider two facts. To begin with, although loans from local (and national) development banks involved subsidized and often even negative real rates of interest for many years, much of the subsidization derived from the tax postponements that were granted. Even in those cases in which the latter were not authorized, investors would not have shown sizable profits initially and thus, would not have incurred large tax obligations to the city and state for several years. The level of public expenditures for which tax revenue would be required in the future was likely be a good deal higher because of some of the "quality-of-life" projects that were being undertaken. Yet the interviews referred to in the reports did not mention any objections by the new investors to the higher level of expenditures and consequently higher level of future local taxes that the enterprises were likely to have to pay after the tax concession periods ended. (Nor were such objections voiced in the more than fifty open-ended interviews with enterprises and private sector consultants that this author conducted in the late 1990s, which are discussed in Chapter 7.) In addition, consider the "natural" economic incentive of less expensive manpower that many companies cited as a reason for establishing a facility in Curitiba. Engineers and technicians as well as laborers and white collar workers earned substantially less in Curitiba for comparable work than in São Paulo and Rio, and somewhat less than in Belo Horizonte and Porto Alegre throughout the entire period from 1970 through the end of the 1990s. In the comparison with São Paulo, the difference may have been of the order of 25-40 percent at the beginning of the period and 20 to 25 percent towards the end. This exceeded the difference between the generally lower cost of living in Curitiba, and the other leading industrial centers, in any event between 1970 and 1990. (By the 1990s the cost of living in Curitiba was higher than in a few of Brazil's other major cities.) Thus, the purchasing power of a given remuneration to a laborer, an engineer or an accountant in Curitiba tended to be somewhat lower than that of an individual of the same skill in São Paulo, Belo Horizonte and Porto Alegre. Either professionals and workers accepted the lesser real income in a specific point of time in exchange for the hope of a significantly higher income in the long run (which in fact they obtained, judging by the greater rise in per capita income in Curitiba), or they were willing to accept the sacrifice in the purchasing power of their remuneration, in exchange for more agreeable living conditions (at least in the short run). The "more agreeable living conditions" refers not only to parks, pedestrian malls, etc., but also to such matters as safer streets due in part to the more effective (and more humane) police protection, moderately better public education, and perhaps better social services, which, seemed, moreover, to be improving more rapidly than in most other communities.

The assumption by some economists that Curitiba's surge in industrialization can be explained simply by the city's proximity to the country's major market coupled with the nature of industrial sprawl and pollution in São Paulo seems highly doubtful.

---

[1]   The five paragraphs that follow draw heavily on Magalhães 1996.

[2]   Unemployment rates are understated in comparison with those in a country like the United States because of the lack of unemployment insurance and therefore a greater tendency of those who lose their regular jobs to seek alternative, even much lower paying positions.

[3]   Much of what follows is taken from Padis 1970 and Augusto 1978.

[4]   See Eakin 2001, especially pages 20-21, 98-106, 129-130, 154-155. One difference was that in Minas Gerais, support of the industrial sector was primarily in iron and steel, drawing on local natural resources (as later, also in bauxite, manganese and phosphates), followed by subsidized support of automobiles, but with the state taking on a role as a promoter and major investor, not just a lender to private enterprise. Another important difference was that the Government of Minas Gerais sought the involvement of foreign capital early on, largely because the projects of greatest attraction required investments much greater than those that *mineiro* businessmen could provide.

[5]   IPARDES April 1980.

[6]   IPARDES September, October and November 1981.

[7]   For indication of the support offered by the State of Minas Gerais from the 1960s through the 1990s, see Eakin 2001, especially pages 3-5, 7, 20-21, 56-57, 60, 62, 75-86, 89-90, 98-103, 106-108, 111-117, 124-126, 129-131, 134-135, 152-156, and 171-172. Eakin maintains that the industrialization of Belo Horizonte and Minas Gerais (indeed, Brazil generally) was "characterized by strong state intervention, political patronage, clientelism, family networks, and a pronounced absence of technological innovation." *Ibid*: 3. He stresses the decisive role of the state government of Minas Gerais and notes that two-thirds of all new industrial investment in Minas Gerais between 1970 and 1977 was generated by the state itself. *Ibid*: 3, 6, 7, 20.

2

Enter Urban Planning

The initial urban plan for Curitiba was proposed by a French urbanist in 1857, and suggestions for improvements in the city's layout date to the period just prior to the First World War, but the first major effort, the Plan Agache, corresponds to the early 1940s. A few words about the latter are in order, but the most notable efforts took place in the mid-1960s. It is this plan—the "Master Plan" (perhaps more accurately, the *Guidelines*), and particularly its implementation, that transformed Curitiba, and changed its image among the cities of Brazil, indeed, among the cities of the world.

The French urbanist, Alfred Agache completed his plan for restructuring the city in 1943. Previously, he had prepared redevelopment proposals for Canberra, Australia, Rio de Janeiro and Santos, the port city of São Paulo State. Curitiba adopted some of his ideas, but hesitated with respect to others. This was fortunate because concepts such as circular boulevards, the series of concentric transportation rings beginning near the heart of the city and spaced at intervals every few kilometers further out (sometimes known as a spoke and wheel design), soon seemed unsuitable. Still, the Agache Plan enabled municipal authorities to better evaluate their situation and provided important suggestions, emphasizing as it did, the alleviation of traffic congestion, improvements in sanitation and flood control, consolidation of government office buildings and the establishment of secondary commercial and social centers beyond the downtown area. Among the specific contributions resulting from the Agache Plan were the improvement of several major traffic arteries, the establishment of new zoning regulations with increased concentration of factories in an Industrial Zone, and the initiation of proposals for the construction of a Civic Center for the state and city governments, a major municipal market, and a new science and engineering campus for the University of Paraná.

The unexpectedly rapid growth of the city, the expanding settlements in what had been rural areas and the presence of terrain that was less suitable for traditional development in certain directions from downtown than others, all began to alter the thinking about what needed to be done. Soon, too, there was another French influence—that of Father Louis Lebret. Father Lebret had first come to Brazil in 1947, and he and his colleagues had prepared studies for São Paulo, Recife and Belo Horizonte. He also had worked in Lebanon, French Indo-China and Africa. His teachings in Curitiba in the 1950s on Economy and Humanism emphasized social concerns as much as physical transformation; they gave a great deal of attention to the quality of urban life—to man as the focus of development planning. Among those influenced by Father Lebret was Ney Braga, who, as mayor in the mid-1950s, created a Department of Urbanism and a Planning Commission that began to explore alternative approaches to the city's development. These ideas and the direction of events in Curitiba were further influenced after 1960 by activities of the state government that already have been mentioned.

The population of Curitiba surged during the 1950s and the 1960s as the State's then dominantly agricultural economy was subjected to major shocks. With Curitiba's population doubling two decades in a row, the available infrastructure was becoming increasingly inadequate, and traffic moved ever more slowly through the once pleasant provincial capital.

Something had to be done. Plans for urban development had been drawn up for one Brazilian city after another—and few were ever taken off the shelves. In the State of Paraná, Governor Ney Braga, seeking to adjust to changing economic conditions and also to dampen secessionist sentiment in the northern part of the state, promoted infrastructure and development-financing institutions aimed at providing alternative economic opportunities to offset the collapsing coffee boom. These factors would have major development consequences for Curitiba. Everyone sought to avoid the problems that had begun to afflict São Paulo, though the possibilities of major industrialization in Curitiba must have seemed remote at that time. Another consideration was to guard against the type of planning for the automobile (rather than for the pedestrian) that characterized Brasilia. Braga felt that the time had come for a new analysis of urbanization in the City of Curitiba.

Mayor Ivo Arzua Pereira's request that CODEPAR finance the extension of a major thoroughfare in Curitiba provided the opportunity. Elected in

1962, Arzua Pereira was troubled with what he characterized as the "urban degeneration" of the city. His concerns were heightened by discussions taking place at the Federal University of Paraná by engineering and architecture students and professors, some of them in the process of organizing the new Faculty of Architecture and Urban Planning. Early in his administration, Arzua created the first municipal low cost housing office in Brazil. His most important decision, however, was to accept the suggestion of Karlos Richbieter that he expand his request for funding to incorporate a comprehensive analysis of urban development possibilities in the city.

Six firms entered into the 1964 competition to devise the new "Indicative" Plan for Curitiba. The successful bidder, Sociedade Serete de Estudos e Projetos Ltd. of São Paulo, undertook the project in collaboration with Arquitetos Associados, headed by Jorge Wilheim. A *Preliminary Plan of Urbanism* was submitted in June 1965. It included an extensive analysis of population and employment growth trends and living conditions in Curitiba, along with projections for the period ahead and their implications for planning and investment. Wilheim, who directed the study, was particularly concerned with the quality of urban life, the alleviation of congestion in the heart of the city, and preservation of the traditional downtown area. He sought a shift from the radial, multiple "beltway" orientation of the earlier Agache Plan to a linear approach, and also counseled that transportation and land use proposals be integrated. The original document was then revised to include two chapters of action proposals. These were prepared by the architects and others from Curitiba who had served as the local counterpart in preparing the analysis.

This *Master Plan* (*Guidelines*) was largely driven by transportation concerns and gave priority to collective over individual transport. It called for the following: 1) linear growth from downtown tangential rapid transit routes that would facilitate a continuous development progression; 2) a hierarchy of routes; 3) preferential development of the city along a Northeast-Southwest axis, consistent with historical and recent spontaneous tendencies; 4) multiple commercial centers; 5) increased urban concentration; 6) extension and improvement of green space; 7) establishment of predominantly pedestrian areas; and 8) creation of a unique urban landscape. The three basic components were attention to land use, the road system and mass transit. (The *Guidelines* also recommended planning at the level of the metropolitan area, farmland until recently, but then beginning to undergo an explosive settlement that was little regulated.) In retrospect, some commentators observed that too little attention was given to the areas prone to flooding, the low bearing capacity of the soils in those areas, and the presence of the major national highway that cut through the city.

While the *Master Plan* broke with the tradition of Brazilian cities of having virtually all traffic intersect in the downtown area, one early commentator maintained that it did not reflect any clear theoretical framework (Fachini 1975). This is noteworthy because of the attention that has been given to Curitiba as an example of successful urban planning. In fact, there has been a great deal of debate—and change—concerning what is involved in the theory of urban planning. According to the English urban planner, Peter Hall, in the late 1950s and early 1960s there was no consistent body of urban planning theory; to the traditional work on land use design, material was added from social or economic planning. Bits and pieces were introduced from sociology and geography as well as economics.[1] Even so, there was an assumption among many planners that it was possible to produce a land use plan that was optimal in some sense. Planning theory was influenced increasingly in the 1960s by applications of location theory from economists and by urban and regional social studies. Walter Isard and others attempted a grand synthesis, promoting a computer-aided systems approach. Eventually, some disenchantment with this led to the reintroduction of politics as well as the social sciences and to more recognition of the role of judgment. "By 1975 Britton Harris, perhaps the most celebrated of all the systems planners, could write that he no longer believed that the more difficult problems of planning could be solved by optimizing methods." (Hall, in Le Gates and Stout 2000: 368). There was increasing resort to what economist/political scientist Charles Lindblom termed incrementalism, perhaps best thought of as a sort of "muddling through." In the 1970s, American and English planners came to be looked upon as informal coordinators employing a new humanistic approach, perhaps not too different than the version of humanism that had begun to influence Curitiba in the 1950s and 1960s.

Hall continues: "Planning, Faludi pointed out in his text of 1973, could be merely *functional*, in that the goals and objectives are taken as given; or normative, in that they are themselves the object of rational choice. The problem was whether planning was really capable of doing that latter job." (*Ibid.*: 370). By the mid-1970s, as the urban planning of Curitiba was in full swing, the theory of urban planning was in a paradigm crisis, with many questioning whether planning had any normative or prescriptive content whatsoever. There was a substantial retreat of practice from theory. A debate continues among urban planners concerning the extent to which urban planning theory should reflect social goals and social theory, and the extent to which an equity component should be determined by objectives or by the process of decision making employed to achieve those objectives (Campbell and Fainstein 1996). One authority states that while planning theory is composed of functional theory and normative theory, no compelling functional theory yet exists. (Lynch in Stein 1995). I would suggest that perhaps the consideration in Curitiba was not so much the theory of urban planning as it was the exposition of a development scheme derived in a consistent manner from a particular vision of urban development.

Whether or not the *Guidelines* prepared Curitiba to meet that test, they are based a great deal on a rule of thumb (judgmental heuristic) that cognitive psychologists term Anchoring and Adjustment (as well as on other heuristics adapted to the particular contexts).[2] The *Guidelines* seem to recognize the difficulty (or impossibility) of a maximizing solution, and to accept the need to resort to judgmental heuristics to get things done. Urban reconstruction seems to have proceeded in an incrementalist manner in Curitiba, but if there is an underlying theory of the urban planning that took place in the city, it is implicit and consists of the way in which the half dozen or more objectives have been advanced. It is a theory of how an overriding vision was implemented—in short, a theory of implementation.

In 1964, a municipal advisory office on urban planning was created, and in late 1965, this was transformed into the Research and Planning Institute of Curitiba (IPPUC), which was given the mission of assuring the implementation of the *Guidelines*. The purpose of this office was similar to one that already existed, but several key individuals in the city's original urban planning unit were transferred to IPPUC, which became a larger and more prominent agency. Several members of this group contributed the chapters in the revised version of the new urban analysis that was submitted in 1966.

A seminar on the industrial development of Curitiba was held in March 1966, and included a large number of organizations and individuals from both the public and private sectors. The principal recommendation was the creation of an Industrial District in a sparsely occupied area of the city used primarily for agriculture and grazing that had been subject to frequent flooding. Earlier, in July 1965, the "Month of Urbanism" had featured a series of meetings and had led to many suggestions and some modifications, but, importantly, the consolidation of citizen support in the community for the type of restructuring that was envisioned. (This "town hall" approach took place two years into the period of military dictatorship, incidentally.) The strongest conclusion that emerged from the 1965 seminar, Curitiba

Tomorrow, was that the city's planning should be integrated, that there should be what later might have been termed a general systems approach. What was intended was not so much systems engineering, but a more ambitious effort to take account of social, economic, and political as well as technological factors. Nonetheless, at least one contemporary commentator complained that the *Guidelines* did not give enough attention to social factors and interdisciplinary analysis (again, Fachini 1975). Architects and others raised a number of criticisms during the public discussions of 1965-66, but they dealt with individual points; no coherent alternative was brought forth. Moreover, as one of those involved in the early implementation of the *Guidelines* maintained, it was not a matter of having the best plan, but of having a plan ready for immediate implementation (Coelho 1974: 23).[3]

Some of the specific recommendations of the *Guidelines* called for a hierarchy of urban routes; avenues to link the major neighborhoods (*bairros*) of the city; the designation of streets and public squares to be given special prominence; the construction of low income housing and community centers; a requirement that there be at least 90 feet of space between apartment houses more than 180 feet tall; special prevision to prevent obstructive construction and garbage deposits in the river beds; urban renewal to revitalize areas in decline; the preservation of historic and traditional sectors; and the designation of areas dedicated to educational and health care institutions.

Approval of the *Guidelines* came at the end of July 1966, and initial advances were made towards fulfilling the objectives outlined even in the few months remaining of the term of office of Mayor Ivo Arzua. The mayor who followed Arzua in office, a sanitary engineer with a degree from Harvard, was particularly concerned with flood control and sewer extensions. He put the more ambitious aspects of the *Guidelines* on hold, but this was not entirely a setback. In the intervening four years, IPPUC was able to examine alternatives for implementing the various objectives of restructuring the city and to discern plausible means for carrying them into effect—initially under the leadership of Jaime Lerner, and then, after the latter's replacement as Director, in large measure with the impetus of his contributions as a highly influential staff member. A number of the IPPUC staff became key members of what later evolved into the politically powerful "Lerner Group."

Jorge Wilheim later held major political positions in the City and State of São Paulo including that of Planning Minister, and was an organizer of the United Nations' Habitat II. His informal remarks at a commemorative session more than thirty years after devising the Curitiba "Master Plan," are most revealing. He characterized his urban planning proposals for the city of

Joinville, Santa Catarina, as more fully developed and innovative than the Curitiba plan developed that same year, as already noted. However, he observed that the work undertaken for Curitiba had included a substantial counterpart group and involved public hearings and debate, while the plan for Joinville had remained on the shelf, largely ignored. Wilheim had contributed to the implementation stage in Curitiba, of course, and had even encouraged discussion about a possible transformation of several blocks of the principal downtown thoroughfare into a pedestrian walkway. The public involvement had another impact. The references to urban planning in Curitiba often suggest that there was a great deal of objectivity involved. From the very beginning, though, what was sought touched on so many objectives that it could not possibly have reflected an optimization process, but rather, a complex of considerations with tradeoffs in objectives and the ways to implement them.[4] This may help explain why, despite references to the involvement of economists and the consideration of economic factors, only two of the nearly fifty persons who contributed to the seven volumes of reminisces about IPPUC were trained as economists (though a number did take short courses on development offered by the Economic Commission for Latin America and the Caribbean —ECLAC).[5] It also may help explain why, except for the transportation system, this urban planning success story has attracted so little attention from economists. (That, along with the strong assumption by many economists that national and regional economic forces must have explained what took place in the economy of Curitiba—that those forces would have provided a rational explanation of what occurred.)

---

[1] Hall, in LeGates and Stout, eds.: 1966: 362-374.

[2] Anchoring and Adjustment is a heuristic or Rule of Thumb that involves an adjustment from a given starting point such as recent historical data or, in this case, the existing development patterns of the city. Anchoring and Adjustment judgments are mental short cuts--short cut alternatives to the types of calculations that aim at achieving what economists have traditionally regarded as the best possible results. Among the biases of those heuristics or mental short cuts are unwarrantedly high levels of confidence. For more on Rules of Thumb, see Appendix A.

[3] The late Herbert Simon, a Nobel laureate in economics as well as professor of psychology and computer science, maintained that it is debatable whether those who attempt to optimize have the best chance of doing so. "In Darwinian theory today it is generally acknowledged that the fitness terrain is very rough, with scads of local maxima. Few population evolutionists claim any more that anything is being optimized-rather that organisms that climb faster

will likely survive better....Ability to move rapidly in new directions may be much more important to survival than optimization, even if that were possible (which it almost never is). And heuristics-especially heuristics that identify new problems and changes in the environment at an early point-may be what is required for rapid adaptation to change." Simon, personal communication, February 10, 1997, quoted from Schwartz 1998, 27, note 8.

[4] Rafael Dely, a prominent member of the Lerner Group over the years, maintained that a city has objective values such as good vehicular circulation, good public transport, living areas and areas for work and leisure activities, but also subjective values such as scale, landscape, liveliness, continuity and memory. Cámara Municipal 1997: Dely, 2.

[5] This contrasts with the experience of Belo Horizonte and Minas Gerais, where most of those who constituted the influential group of technocrats were trained as engineers in the 1930s and 1940s, but as economists after 1960. Eakin 2001: 153-154. (Throughout his study, Eakin also gives attention to the fact that many of the technocrats came from the ranks of the elite families of Minas Gerais. In Curitiba, sons of immigrants occupied the leadership of the technocrat group and many of their collaborators were from a middle class background rather than from the Paraná elite.) Another difference between the experience of the two metropolitan areas is that while Curitiba's urban plan was prepared prior to major industrialization and greatly influenced the city's subsequent development, that drawn up for Greater Belo Horizonte six years later, came after the area's industrialization was well underway, and judging by the only passing reference to it in Eakin's study of industrialization in the city, was of much less consequence.

3

Implementing the *Guidelines*, 1966-1982

Introduction

The *Master Plan* analyzes the situation in Curitiba in the mid-1960s, pro-vides projections for the years ahead, and then sets forth a wide ranging set of guidelines. It brings together a great deal of material and incorporates several surveys undertaken specifically for this effort. The key population projections, while high for 1990 and 2000, were very nearly on target for 1980. Three estimates were offered for that year: a high of 2,100,000; a middle of 1,400,000; and a low estimate of 830,000. The actual figure turned out to be 1,025,000. This meant that the resources sought to initiate the recommended urban restructuring (which were obtained) might have exceeded what was required by a small margin. Although most of the fi-nancing came from the state and city governments, financial support was abetted by the favor with which the military government looked upon the experiment in Curitiba, in part, perhaps because it was led by an individual with a technical rather than traditional political background.

Although many agencies of the municipal government would be involved in implementing the *Guidelines*, principal responsibility rested with IPPUC and URBS, the Urbanization Company of Curitiba, which was established in 1968. IPPUC would be responsible for the supervision of planning and dissemination of information about the process, as well as administration and implementation. URBS would manage the public facilities of the city. The concepts of the *Guidelines* and the blueprint follow-ups were elabo-rated more fully in IPPUC, with hands-on implementation of projects undertaken by URBS (and CIC, the industrial city, which was spun off from URBS). Some activities were undertaken by the existing Municipal Secretariat of Urban Development, but IPPUC became preeminent among the three agencies, certainly as of 1971. Several secretariats of the State Government sometimes collaborated closely with municipal authorities, and from the date of its establishment in 1974, IPARDES, the Institute of Economic and Social Development of the State of Paraná provided background studies and contemporary analyses that were often utilized by city planners. Many leading officials and staff members shifted back and forth between various agencies that dealt with the redevelopment of Curitiba over the course of their careers. Special commissions with both public and private sector members advised on a number of topics. Staff members of city and state agencies were encouraged, and in many cases, given financial support to enroll in various training programs—notably foreign (especially French) programs in urban and regional planning, local Master's degree programs, and shorter ECLA courses on economic development. Enterprises took advantage of the incentive mechanisms of the State of Paraná where possible, but explicit budgetary support provided the principal resources for the urban renovation of Curitiba, with the state and city, partners in the major large loan used to fund CIC.

The Municipality of Curitiba officially approval the *Guidelines* on July 31, 1966. Some initial advances were made towards fulfilling the objectives in the remaining months of outgoing Mayor Arzua's term of office but his successor, Omar Sabbag, had a somewhat different agenda, as already noted. That Administration did begin work on zoning regulations and land use, however. A dispute over a proposed new bus and railroad station led Jaime Lerner, the architect/urban planner who headed up IPPUC, to step down from formal leadership of the institute. Nonetheless, he remained on as a staff member and provided the leadership in examining the alternatives for implementing the *Guidelines*. Discussions about urban planning options continued, but more were held behind closed doors than at the time the *Guidelines* first came to the public's attention in 1965.

Transportation, Linear Growth and Land Use

The events of 1965-66 reflected a widely felt expression of hope for a revitalized, more livable city. The debates were primarily about the details of how best to achieve that objective. What would differentiate Curitiba from other cities for which plans had been drawn up would be the degree of commitment that followed—on the part of the city, the state, and perhaps most important, on the part of the local counterpart professionals who had worked with the outside experts in drawing up the *Guidelines*.

The initial commitment of the City of Curitiba, beginning with the establishment of IPPUC, has already been noted. That was reaffirmed in 1970-71. In late 1970, Ney Braga, the former Mayor of Curitiba, Congressman, Governor of Paraná, and subsequently, national Minister of Agriculture and Minister of Education and Culture, as well as President of Itaipu, the world's largest hydroelectric generating plant, urged the then Governor of the State to designate Jaime Lerner to be Mayor of Curitiba. The chief magistrate of the city was not to be an experienced political figure, but the 33-year-old "technician" most closely identified with the campaign for the city's restructuring. (For a biography of Jaime Lerner, see Appendix B.)

The first measures implementing the *Guidelines* (those for which Curitiba is perhaps best known internationally), dealt with transportation. Drawing at least as much from the historical development of Curitiba as from any concepts of urban planning, and attempting to assure order in the city's future patterns of growth, the *Guidelines* called for preferential development along a Northeast-Southwest axis, with this linear growth served by rapid transit routes. Conceivably that might have been warranted by careful calculation, but such was not offered. The recommended approach reflected the use of an Anchoring and Adjustment Rule of Thumb. Another objective was to develop a transportation system with terminals spread throughout the city, not just at one or two points downtown. The intent was to avoid having everything converge on the historic center of Curitiba, thus helping to preserve its attraction while at the same time, minimizing congestion. This was important given the continuing reliance on surface transport, but it was remarkable for a city still quite small by international standards.

In comments to the author, Jaime Lerner wrote:

The Master Plan had on its guidelines, linear growth along the Northeast-Southwest axis, induced by the transportation system. What it didn't predict was the trinitarian [three lane] system. Well, the initial plan, with rapid lanes next to the bus lane, would have been too expensive, since we would have had to spend a lot of money on expropriations in order to enlarge the streets parallel to the axis that could be perfectly used as rapid transit routes. We saved public money and did something simple. Lerner 2003.

Trolley cars dominated public transportation in Curitiba from 1887 through the late 1940s, but buses, which had been in circulation since 1928, became the major means of public locomotion in the 1950s. The variety of types of vehicles, the many narrow streets and the disinclination of the many private companies to service low population density areas all led the city to reorganize the public transit system in the mid-1950s. That brought a measure of improvement but with the rapid growth of Curitiba in that decade and the next, something more was required. Indeed, mounting traffic and public transportation problems were the driving force behind the effort to get a new plan for urban development.

Although the *Guidelines* provided an indication of what was recommended, little was actually implemented in the four years before Lerner became mayor. Charles Wright, the transportation economist who analyzed Curitiba's transportation proposals for the Inter-American Development Bank in the 1990s, wrote of the city he had seen in 1970:

> In the late 1960s, Curitiba's infrastructure was overwhelmed, and there was a danger of a collapse in its services…The central grid of streets was overrun by cars and buses, and the noise and fumes from stop-and-go traffic, invaded the shops and other establishments. The older buildings were showing signs of neglect and abandonment. Pressures were mounting to engage in a major road-building exercise to make more room for cars and reduce congestion, despite the failure of similar efforts in other…cities around the world. Wright 1996a.

With Lerner in office, the changes proceeded in earnest. IPPUC had prepared a general transportation study in 1968-69 which considered trolleys and also an underground metro but decided in favor of bus transportation as the more economical. Most of the first stage details had been worked out by 1972, and construction was initiated in 1973, with full implementation of the system under way by 1974. The city would oversee public transportation more actively than before, but private companies would continue to own and operate the vehicles. Buses were rerouted, express buses were introduced and shelters with fiberglass roofs were set up. There would be several major arteries, each with two lanes exclusively for buses in the center and one-way local traffic on either side. Parallel to those major transit axes, flanking them a block to the left and to the right, there would be one-way streets facilitating faster movement of private traffic. This three street approach to the major transportation flows took advantage of existing traffic arteries and thus avoided having to make large expenditures for expropriations and road construction, particularly in the initial period.

At first, the great majority of the bus lines linked the center city with the various neighborhoods, but over time, more buses provided direct connections between the neighborhoods. Additional regional terminals were established (some of them, cement and brick structures with steel roofs), and more of the feeder bus lines ended in those terminals. With this, the system became more integrated and it was possible to travel to more destinations within the city without paying a second fare. In addition, the terminals were developed as small commercial centers, many with branch offices of municipal government departments. In 1980, the single fare for the integrated system was instituted, subsidizing the longer trips that many low-income residents were obliged to make. From the beginning, city officials indicated the special characteristics of the buses that were to be used, and negotiated with Cummins, Mercedes and Volvo in increasingly successful attempts to get them to produce vehicles with the specifications they sought. As of 1980, there were 761 kilometers in the integrated bus network, including 56 kilometers of exclusive bus lanes.

The emerging and continuously evolving transportation setup had a good deal going for it. A prerequisite was that it had to meet cost-benefit criteria to qualify for loans from the World Bank in the 1970s and 80s and from the IDB in the 1990s. In the late 1960s, in the early 1980s, and again at the end of that decade, consideration was given to alternatives to buses for public transport. Note was taken of the cost-effectiveness of a bus system that could be upgraded periodically at relatively little cost to the public sector, and of the budget constraint. The latter refers to the inability to gain access to the much higher level of funding required for alternative transportation options.[1] The use of more than a dozen bus terminals to avoid having an excessive amount of traffic intersect downtown made sense, but that decision seems to have reflected a combination of the strongly voiced preferences of political leaders and back-of-the-envelope calculations. Other measures taken over the years to cope with both new and anticipated difficulties reflected pragmatic responses to remedy problems at hand. Copies of Walter Isard's text on regional economics can be found in the IPUUC library, but they do not reveal the signs of wear and tear that one would expect had they been consulted extensively. World Bank analyses of transportation loans for Curitiba may have included some economic modeling, but overall, it appears that even this most internationally applauded achievement in one of the most successful socioeconomic urban renewals of the last generation did not involve many optimization calculations. Even so, the Rules of Thumb and "pragmatic responses" worked; the evolution of public transportation in Curitiba proved better than efforts in many cities that were more along the lines that most economists and financial analysts feel comfortable with.[2]

Curitiba's emphasis on the Northeast-Southwest corridor and subsequently on four other major traffic arteries was intended to orient municipal growth and to encourage higher density housing (particularly high rise construction) alongside those arteries. Increased population density would facilitate economies of scale in housing, provide a demand for better and more frequent bus service, and with that, enable a modern transportation system using exclusive bus lane arrangements to be financially viable. Zoning guidelines were laid down for the type of residences and businesses that would be permitted in various parts of the city in an effort to assure orderly development, most notably in 1972 and 1975. This reflected an updated and more systematic version of the approach to the zoning initiated by Ney Braga in the 1950s. The spatial specifications reflected a rough logic, but also a certain measure of arbitrariness. A tendency was observed to take account of *de facto* situations in drawing up regulations, as will become clearer in the chapters that follow. No explanations were offered for the precise boundaries of land use that were specified, nor were there discussions of the tradeoffs involved or the alternatives that were considered and rejected. It has been claimed that there was more respect for the zoning regulations in Curitiba than in São Paulo and Rio, and while that might seem to bode well for the city's development, changing circumstances might have called for variations in land use regulations, all the more so because, however satisfactory, those regulations probably had some margin for improvement to begin with.

High rise apartments sprung up that failed to meet the *Guidelines* recommendations for living space between buildings, however, and not only on the streets immediately adjacent to the principal transportation axes. Nor were there many small parks between buildings, as had been urged (and anticipated). A system of transfer of building rights evolved whereby individuals could purchase development rights (notably the right to increase the density of their developments) with the funds paid being used to finance the preservation of open spaces and historic buildings or the construction of low income housing. Critics asserted that the construction industry obtained many exceptions from the spatial and other recommendations of the *Guidelines* and that these exceptions involved insider connections and irregularities but those allegations were rarely accompanied by specifics. More and more, tall condominiums began to replace the simple but attractive pine wood homes that had long been typical of Curitiba. Despite the color and attractive style of some of the new structures, the face of the city began to change in a manner that few had expected. There were many public expressions of regret about the trend, but the silent majority kept on buying or renting the new apartments that came on the market and continued to show enthusiasm for their dwellings. It was not until many years later that measures finally were taken to require more space between buildings and a closer adherence to the mandates of the *Guidelines* (though by that time much had changed and new mandates might have been appropriate). The truth is that the *Guidelines* left much to the discretion of municipal authorities, though perhaps wisely so, given the dynamics of development.

Downtown

The new municipal administration, with leaders who were primarily architects, urban planners and engineers, moved energetically to make Curitiba a more attractive, livable community. To begin with, downtown would not be cluttered with vehicles; rather, it would be dedicated to pedestrians—a reaction against what was taking place in Brasilia. One Friday evening, early in the first Lerner Administration, unannounced, the pavement of five blocks along 15th of November Street, the principal commercial thoroughfare of the city, was ripped up and transformed over the course of the next few days into an attractive pedestrian mall, complete with benches, trees and other plantings. Howls of protest from merchants followed, but they were promised that the change would be reversed after six months if they were still in disagreement.[3] (The notion of making this pedestrian mall was not new; the suggestion had first been made by Jorge Wilheim, the coordinator of the *Guidelines*, during the public meetings of 1965.) That same trend continued until a decade later there were twenty city blocks in the center of the city's principal commercial area in which the use of vehicles was severely circumscribed—the largest downtown pedestrian mall in absolute as well as relative terms in all the world. The city's principal street, once very much the vehicular snarl described by transportation economist Charles Wright, had become "The Street of Flowers." An IPPUC architect captured the spirit of what was being done, declaring, "…the street must no longer be only an avenue, but a great square where people can come together and enjoy life."[4] Few economists or financial analysts would have endorsed such an extended pedestrian mall, completely dominating the downtown business district, but the city seems to have gained by having made downtown so pedestrian-friendly. The local businesses were rejuvenated and continued to thrive. Gradually, many other Brazilian cities (even São Paulo) began to follow the example of Curitiba, though on a much smaller scale.

Other developments downtown also were controversial. The *Guidelines* enunciate a commitment to preserving the historic center of the city, and while "modern street widening" was avoided and preservation was undertaken, some critics contend that a number of important structures were unnecessarily demolished (to facilitate road construction and overpasses).

The strongest objections have been aimed at the city's approval in 1980, of a large shopping center in an abandoned metalworking plant that occupied two city blocks midway between the historic downtown area and the then, newly constructed, modernistic buildings of the state and city governments. As background, note that the traditional downtown merchants had been placated by the success in transforming several blocks of 15th of November Street into a pedestrian mall, Curitiba was booming in the late 1970s, and there was a growing demand for more upscale merchandising. Enter the proposed Mueller Shopping Center project.

Three objections were raised against the project.

First, the large structure in which the metalworking plant had been located was in a zone in which historic structures were to be preserved and only small-to-medium size commercial establishments were to be authorized. In a recent book, historian Dennison de Oliveira contends that the city did not follow proper legal procedures in approving the Miller Shopping Center project, basing part of his argument on the conclusions of investigations conducted by the administration and city council that took office after the Lerner Group, in late 1982-83. (Oliveira 2000) (Note that those officials were overwhelmingly political opponents of the Lerner Group.) In addition, concerns were raised about the traffic that the shopping center would generate, adding to an already congested area. Finally, objectors claimed that the same traffic concerns and the legal points noted by Oliveira already had led to rejection of one proposal to transform the structure into a shopping center; the only significant difference, they claimed, was that those involved in the second proposal were friends of the mayor.

While I was unable to ascertain certain details concerning the controversy, several points should be noted. First, while the former factory may not have been an architectural gem, outside observers acknowledge that it was a unique structure in Brazil. One of the points at issue is whether the shopping mall proposal envisioned a preservation of the building's façade and utilization of the interior space as restricted as that which was required by the historical preservation law. Second, although the proposal included parking facilities within the building, that did not completely eliminate traffic concerns. Third, the earlier proposal for a shopping mall would have established a huge discount store in dramatic violation of the zoning requirements, particularly those concerning store size. The proposal that was approved anticipated small to medium size establishments, primarily of merchants already well established in the city. Moreover, in many cases, stores would be of a higher category than that of the rejected discount chain. The latter was ultimately constructed—just outside the city limits of Curitiba—and it has been a commercial success in that location. Meanwhile, the new Miller Shopping Center helped Curitiba's downtown continue as the most important commercial and social center of the city long after the traditional downtown areas of several other large Brazilian cities had deteriorated quite badly.

The precedent of the Miller Shopping Center facilitated subsequent approval of a number of other relatively close-in shopping malls, several nearer to each other than anticipated by zoning regulations, and at least one of which was also subject to other objections. Traffic increased greatly, though perhaps not much more than one would expect in the major commercial areas of a large city. Most residents of Curitiba appreciate the presence of these shopping malls—the Rules of Thumb used to make the planning decisions were serviceable and accepted by the community—but the criteria for shopping mall approval and the implementation of existing zoning regulations in Curitiba have not been entirely transparent.

Parks, Green Space and Flood Control

At least as profound was the impact from the change in Curitiba's approach to flood control. Much of the city had been subject to inundation, even the very heart of downtown. In the past, the banks of some rivers had been cemented in the most heavily populated areas. This was expensive and also created problems downstream. At that point, perhaps in part because the most urgent channelization had been completed, but also because of advances in understanding how to deal with flooding, the city adopted a new approach. Flood plains and other possibly vulnerable terrain were transformed into parks and forest preserves that would absorb much of the rainwater run-offs and slow their return to the streams, while, at the same time, also channeling a portion of the water into newly created (or expanded) lake basins.

The result was to expand the area of public parks and forests more than twenty-fold per capita and to provide locales attractive enough to draw large numbers of people from all segments of the city's population. Twenty-six major parks were created, one of which was the largest urban park in all Latin America. Most of these combination recreation/flood control projects were located away from the center of the city, where they were as accessible to those who lived in lower income neighborhoods further out as to those who lived closer in. However, through much of the 1970s and early 1980s the policy of "benign neglect" in dealing with river runoffs in much of the southern part of the city continued. It was felt that those lands ought to remain very low-density areas and the city avoided installing much urban infrastructure even as these formerly marginal farmlands became much more heavily populated. While it now seems obvious that the much needed flood control and the almost equally sought park space could be resolved synergistically, that does not appear to have occurred to many people before 1970.[5] Once this means of achieving the two objectives by the same means became recognized, the ease of explaining it compared to the difficulty of grasping complex hydraulic solutions also contributed to its political attractiveness, as noted in a seminar held at the IDB in 1996.

Reflecting on the way in which the city dealt with the areas subject to river runoffs, Lerner later observed:

The social issue is always used as an excuse to allow occupation near the rivers, but the truth is the costs they impose are always very high, more than the investments necessary to provide dignified housing. If any occupation should exist by the rivers, streams and the rear of valleys, with risk of flooding, it has to be an intelligent occupation with advantage for the entire population and in harmony with nature. For example, occupying these places with leisure or sports areas, with vegetation. These areas don't have to be considered only for preservation, but they might have an important utilization for the population. Many times, it is exactly the right use that allows preservation.

With this kind of usage, and not with housing or essential equipment, if one day there is a flood in these areas, the only problem is that the ducks will swim in a bigger pool. Curitiba adopted largely this tool. In big parks as well as in bikeways by the rivers or in small leisure areas. Instead of trying to measure the city for the next flood, when most of the time there is no money to solve the basic problems, it is necessary to anticipate the expansion of the city and to avoid the multiplication of problems. Lerner 2003.

Neighborhood Centers, Low Income Projects, and Coordination of the Metropolitan Area

There was some concern that the heart of the city not be overemphasized, and the *Guidelines* mentioned the objective of developing secondary neighborhood centers but did not indicate how to go about this. The increasing number of new transportation terminals led to a gradual development of a number of neighborhood centers, though further impetus of the municipality along those lines was less in the years through 1982 than some had hoped for.

Low income housing and the concern with socially oriented projects emerged slowly. At the level of the State Government, little was done until the second half of the 1970s, when, for example, the State Administration of Jayme Canet Junior, made safe drinking water directly available to 90 percent of the residents of Curitiba. Low-income housing was not mentioned in the *Guidelines*, and may not have seemed like a pressing need until late in the 1970s. The first significant steps were taken by Jaime Lerner's designated successor, Saul Raiz. Several slums of little more than one hundred persons each were demolished and their residents relocated to sites of new popular housing. In addition, self-construction projects were initiated. The National Mortgage Bank financed much of the lower income housing and the weight of architects in the city administration finally succeeded in moving away from the ultra-standardized housing by the second Lerner Administration of 1979-82. Rafael Dely, head of Curitiba's housing agency, presided over the construction of 40,000 units during the period 1976-83. Even so, center-left political opponents criticized him for being overly concerned with quality at a time when the unfulfilled need for basic housing was accelerating.

Public health assistance also began to be given more attention in the second Lerner Administration, and even an active member of the opposition Worker's Party characterized Jaime Lerner as a Brazilian pioneer in that field. Public nurseries for working mothers were initiated in this period under Lerner and Raiz, though on a reduced scale.

The first two major objectives of the Metropolitan Curitiba Region Authority dealt with the preservation of natural resources and wealth generation (primarily what was termed "industrial dynamics"), neither of which is closely related to the other topics in this section. However, the third concern of the metropolitan authority, the creation of regional sub-centers with urban services, clarifies the connection. It was in the area outside the city limits of Curitiba that most newcomers to the metropolitan region first settled, and it was there that incomes and living standards were lowest. The nature of the problems was not clear to many of the leaders in Curitiba at first, though, and progress came slowly in coordinating the activities of the metropolitan area.

The Reasoning and Readjustments

By the late 1970s-early 1980s Curitiba already had gained a measure of fame. Several Brazilian MA theses on urban planning focused on the city. The World Bank had begun to finance Curitiba's approach to public transportation.[6] The change in the city continued to meet some resistance, however. A number of bus owners objected to the new regulations concerning public transit, some landowners in areas being expropriated for the Industrial City brought suits against the municipality for what they believed was inadequate compensation, preservationists objected to the destruction of several historic buildings, complaints were voiced about a lack of attention to housing in and around CIC, and some long-time Curitiba businessmen expressed resentment for not receiving incentives as generous as those accorded new investors. There were complaints from both the right and the left.

The economic rejuvenation of Curitiba began halfway through the period of the Brazilian miracle (1968-73). In the early 1970s, the national banks were quite receptive to requests from Curitiba, which government leaders in Brasilia viewed as an outstanding example of a rational approach to city planning. By 1974-75, Brazil, which imports the overwhelming portion of its petroleum, was rocked by the tremendous hikes in fuel prices. The country attempted to grow its way out of the energy crisis, borrowing petrodollars from abroad and continuing many of the projects originally planned. During this period Paraná probably faired better than average for the country, perhaps in part because of the additional socioeconomic transformation it was undergoing. The vast Itaipú hydroelectric project, at the western edge of the state, on the border with Paraguay, was ushered in at the beginning of the crisis, and towards the end of the decade, the Metropolitan Curitiba Region was successful in attracting a major government oil refinery. The first was justified largely in traditional economic terms (even if there were questions about how it was financed). The second reflected the State's growing political significance. In addition, Paraná was a beneficiary of Brazil's controversial gasohol program, emerging as a new producer of sugar. In short, while Brazilian growth and the inflow of new foreign investment slowed during the period beginning 1974 and financing became more expensive, the State of Paraná and the City of Curitiba were not as suddenly disadvantaged as some other regions in their attempt to attract new industry. Curitiba did suffer from a general disadvantage in its attempts to attract foreign enterprises; it lacked the number and quality of industrial suppliers and training institutions which most new investors from abroad or even from São Paulo were accustomed to having accessible. But while the Brazilian boom seemed to be slowing down somewhat, Curitiba was beginning to bask in the lights as a city that had found a way to grow and to do so with an improved quality of life. The key question, then, is how Curitiba achieved this. What were the criteria of the urban planning guidelines and their implementation?

One of the first evaluations of the Curitiba experience was presented in an M.A thesis on urban planning prepared for the Federal University of Rio de Janeiro, based principally on the basis of materials available in IPPUC in 1974. (Fachini 1975) The author affirmed that the much-hailed *Plano Diretor* lacked a theoretic framework, as has been noted. Another study two years later, attributed the success of Curitiba's experience to the establishment of a strong planning organization (IPPUC), the involvement of the mayor in the planning process, an incrementalist strategy (as opposed to a strongly methodological approach) and yet laws that were said to minimize the role of discretion (IUPERJ 1977). An urban planning thesis written for the University of London a decade later contended that what makes Curitiba a special case is not the content of the plan, "but the transformation and utilization of such content as basic guidelines for policy formation"—the implementation of the plan, with attention to the political aspects of planning (Quandt 1985). Revealing are the observations of Lubomir Ficinski, one of the leading members of the Lerner Group and, for a number of years, an urban development consultant for the World Bank. In 1989, reflecting on all that had happened, he remarked, "We did things intuitively, and now, looking back it can be seen that we were learning while doing." (*Memoria da Curitiba Urbana* 1989). (Support for such a pragmatic approach was voiced by Jaime Lerner himself in a comment made in 2003 that is cited later in this text.) It is likely that the intuitive manner that Ficinski refers to and with which Lerner expressed agreement, involved a judicious mixture of decision rules, optimization techniques and improvisation by people with a profound knowledge of the city and an accumulating experience that helped gauge what tended to work in given situations, and what did not. Unfortunately, there are no accounts available of the specific manner in which any of the major issues were resolved. The 1982 studies of IPPUC outlining accomplishments and setting forth new proposals also neglect to indicate the rationale for determining the particular proposals that were recommended (rather than some other variation of that mix).

Part of the reason why the implementation of the *Master Plan* had such an impact may well be because the guidelines were modified along the way, in no small measure to take account of the city's interest groups, picking up political and economic support as activities progressed.[7] Yet this has also been part of the criticism of the process (Oliveira 2000), as has been noted, especially from the center-left political opposition, though also from many apolitical individuals such as those at the Federal University of Paraná.

---

[1] This is taken from comments made by Charles Wright in March 2001 to an earlier draft of this study.

[2] For detail on the measures taken in the area of transportation over the years see del Santoro 2000, Unknown Compiler 1999 and Ceneviva [1999?].

[3] Lerner notes:

The pedestrian mall was accomplished in 72 hours. I still remember that when the project was announced, the reaction of the business owners was contrary and very strong. We knew that the idea would be difficult to implement, for the works could be stopped by lawsuits. So it was imperative to do the work fast, very fast. The completion date anticipated by my Secretary of Public Works was a few months, at least. I insisted on 48 hours. I am sure that they thought I was crazy. The Secretary came to me to say that the work could be done in a month. I refused it once again, and so new suggestions on how to implement the project faster began to appear: to get the furniture in advance; special work teams to set the sidewalks in each block. And so the time was being reduced, and the Secretary told me: one week. I refused and got an agreement that it would be done in 72 hours. We would start on a Friday night and the work would be completed and delivered to the public on Monday night. Should the people not approve the change, we could always go back to what was there before. But it was necessary for the population to see the finished product. And this is how it was done.

The day that followed the dedication, one of the business owners that headed the petition against the project, came to me with another request: the same should be done to include other areas. Sometimes, urban acupuncture requires quick and precise insertions. Lerner 2003.

4   Assad 1973. He went on to list the functions that could be developed in the street as social, cultural and political as well as economic.

5   However, see IPARDES January/April 1995.

6   See especially del Santoro 2000.

7   Eakin notes the role of three powerful interest groups in shaping the process of industrialization in Minas Gerais–politicians, technocrats and entrepreneurs. Eakin 2001: 4-5.

4

Curitiba's Industrial City

The principal concerns of the mid-1960s *Plano Diretor* were public transportation, the relief of traffic congestion, a more pedestrian-friendly and attractive downtown, parks and flood control. The *Guidelines* referred to the desirability of a separate industrial district, primarily because of the smoke, fumes and noise from existing processing plants near downtown and from the threat that increases in manufacturing might pose for the quality of life in the city. This was still a secondary concern at the time, however. With the decline of coffee cultivation and the accentuated migration from rural areas to Curitiba in the second half of the 1960s and the decade of the 1970s, there was mounting concern about providing new economic momentum and new sources of employment. A need was sensed to give greater impetus to industrialization and to do so without creating the problems of the existing industrial centers of Brazil—problems that already had occupied the attention of several members of the incoming municipal administration because of their involvement in urban rehabilitation studies of other Brazilian cities. By 1971 the Lerner Group recognized that the directives of the *Guidelines* concerning industry had to be amplified.

Acting almost as if they were unaware that many Latin American industrial parks had turned out to be White Elephants because of a lack of attention to basic economic considerations, the new municipal administration began to think about an innovative industrial district that would feature an extensive expanse of green and occupy a tenth of the entire city. (This is an area approximately a third the size of Baltimore, Maryland and 40 percent as large as Washington, D. C., much larger than the *Cidade Industrial* on the outskirts of more industrialized Belo Horizonte.) Increased consideration of an industrial district also was stimulated by BADEP's consideration in 1971-72, of the proposals presented by several prominent European enterprises to locate manufacturing plants in Curitiba. The attention given to those foreign investors represented a clear break from the 1960s tendency to lend to relatively small firms of local origin that would produce for the local market.

IPPUC set to work, and once again the city turned to the architectural and urban planning group of Jorge Wilheim in São Paulo for assistance. In 1972 Curitiba decided to move ahead with the plans for the Curitiba Industrial City (CIC), to be located in the then sparsely populated western to southwestern part of the city.

With so much terrain that was either hilly or subject to flooding, virtually all of which was privately held, the city had its work cut out for itself. The federal government cooperated by modifying its southern highway trajectory, and also may have assisted in other ways, as two individuals from Curitiba (Karlos Richbieter and Maurício Schulmann) assumed positions of prominence in national financial matters during the 1970s. The commitment of the state government was important throughout the decade—beginning with the leadership of the governor early in the 1970s, and continuing, not only through direct financial support, but also in the activities of the state's public utilities. TELEPAR provided studies and assistance that was influential in the decision of two of the first major foreign investments to locate in the new industrial community. COPEL, the electric power company, constructed the requested power stations, and, acting in conjunction with the Federal University of Paraná, established an electronics laboratory to supplement the activities of TECPAR, the Technological Institute of Paraná, which, at the time, was still primarily oriented to agriculture. And BADEP became even more active in financing industrial enterprises.

First and foremost came the tasks of grading and drainage, and the expropriations of private land. URBS, which was in charge, was allocated nearly a third of the city's budget in the early years. Financing also came from the State Bank, BANESTADO, and a group of private financial institutions. Initially, the State returned a portion of certain taxes it collected to Curitiba's Development Fund to help pay off debts incurred in funding CIC, but this appears to have been a gentleman's agreement and led to differences of interpretation and consequent repayment problems by the beginning of the 1980s.

Questions have been raised with respect to the speed with which the extensive infrastructure of CIC was developed. (The State of Minas Gerais also had leveled grounds, laid out streets and provided other infrastructure in an industrial park adjacent to Belo Horizonte three decades earlier, but that site was much smaller and did not become fully occupied until only a few years before CIC was initiated.) The doubts arose in part because some high-density areas of the city lacked sanitation and road improvements, but particularly because at first only a handful of major corporations indicated an interest in establishing major investments in Curitiba. For a number of years CIC was derided by some critics as the world's largest golf course. Was there too quick a response to merely "visionary" ideas? Did it reflect the extension of special favor to the construction industry and real estate speculators, some perhaps with insider ties? And if the expropriation of farmland and isolated homesteads was fair, why were there so many legal actions by those whose land was taken?

Whether there was an effort to favor special interests or not, as some have charged (see, e. g., Oliveira 2000, esp. 173-75), economists and financial analysts probably would take issue with the rate of discount implicit in the expropriations and infrastructure development undertaken by Curitiba in the 1970s. It is true that given the recession of the mid-1980s and the disinclination of the opposition political groups then in power to provide much additional support for the industrial city (even for the maintenance of existing infrastructure), Curitiba would not have been in a position to accommodate the revealed interest of foreign and domestic investors in the late 1980s and 1990s had there not been the extensive expansion of infrastructure expansion in the 1970s. That, by itself, does not justify the reasoning followed in the 1970s, of course. The case for the 1970s activity may be sufficient only because it must have been recognized that the industrial decentralization of Brazil was certain to continue, and the greatest gains were likely to go to those communities that were in the best condition to receive modern new industries.

In commenting to the questions raised above, Jaime Lerner responds, "Let the numbers answer that. The once-called world's largest golf course is responsible today for 200,000 jobs, with 700 companies installed and 20% of all state exports." Lerner 2003.

Educational institutions and training facilities are critical for the success of a major industrial center. Curitiba had the Federal University of Paraná, the smaller but expanding Catholic University, both with engineering and business administration faculties and programs in the basic sciences. It also possessed CEFET, a federal technical institute that was oriented to secondary and post-secondary education. Public secondary school education, while not truly outstanding, probably was better than in leading industrial communities in Rio Grande do Sul such as Caixias do Sul. Within two years of the initiation of the industrial city, SENAI, the national technical assistance organization, agreed to set up a training facility for workers within the industrial city. TECPAR, the technical assistance arm of the State of Paraná, constructed its headquarters in CIC, and in the 1980s the City of Araucária, just southwest of Curitiba, donated land to establish a middle level technical institute. In addition, there were several other institutes, a second Catholic university just outside the city limits, even a technical school for sanitation needs, the only one in Latin America. Curitiba came to have an increasingly solid educational base for manufacturing industry and would not need to draw extensively upon the educational resources of other cities except for certain specialties.

Inasmuch as CIC was relatively isolated from the historic population center of the city, the construction of major arteries to the heart of the city was imperative and this led to five "connectors." The innovative public transportation system with its subsidized fares for those traveling from a distance provided major assistance. In addition, it was anticipated that housing for low to middle income wage earners would be constructed within CIC or in adjacent areas also zoned for industry. Several of the earliest group of new initial foreign investors were particularly anxious to see this accomplished. Public housing did evolve, though little of it before CIC was into its second year of existence. However, between 1976 and 1983, 40,000 units were made available (with only limited support from the National Mortgage Bank after 1980). While that should have been enough to accommodate all of the workers in the new manufacturing plants, not all sought to live there and many others chose to live in those quarters while working elsewhere.

The favorable response of major investors from elsewhere in Brazil and from abroad was attributable to several factors—natural economic factors to begin with and special incentives to be sure, but also the imaginative promotion of both of those factors. Within Brazil, Curitiba was beginning to gain a measure of fame even in the early to mid 1970s. This served to bring the city to the attention of those thinking about new plant sites and led them to first give serious consideration to Curitiba. Indeed, prior to the publicity about the apparently successful urban restructuring of the city, Curitiba simply did not register as a site to consider for new industry. The major population centers of the country and the medium-size communities in the State of São Paulo and southern Minas Gerais all seem like more serious contenders for new manufacturing plants. The same held for two cities in Santa Catarina that were smaller and further from the major São Paulo market, Joinville and Blumenau, but which resonated among those thinking of modern industry. Curitiba, the university community, state bureaucratic center, and home of lumber companies, furniture makers and Paraguay tea processors, did not.

The promotion within Brazil took several forms. First, Mayor Jaime Lerner and his associates spoke to groups outside Curitiba and welcomed media commentators who prepared increasingly glowing write-ups about the city. Second, former Governor Ney Braga became Minister of Agriculture, Senator and then Minister of Education, and could be counted on to speak out for Curitiba in Brasilia and Rio de Janeiro. Similarly with respect to Karlos Richbieter and Maurício Schulmann, who were appointed to head up national public banks, Richbieter also becoming Minister of Finance of Brazil for the period 1979-81. Beyond this background publicity, BADEP and URBS scheduled investment promotion missions in Brazil and abroad—to Europe, the United States, Canada and Japan. The language facility of many of those who participated in the missions helped—English, German, Italian, Japanese, and various other languages. To jump ahead to the mid-1990s, the familiarity of so many of the Curitiba negotiators with the French language, French culture, and indeed, with France itself, appears to have been a consideration in the decision of Renault to locate there. When those considering Curitiba visited the city, they were greeted with well prepared, technologically up-to-date materials and with responses to their questions, often provided in the languages of the prospective investors. The negotiators from Curitiba clearly meant to outdo rival suitors from more established industrial centers such as Belo Horizonte, Porto Alegre, and Rio de Janeiro.

Curitiba finally was being considered. What did the city have to offer besides its more or less proximate location to the São Paulo market (and its acceptable educational facilities)?

To begin with, the unusually conceived and accelerated construction of CIC provided a signal that this formerly traditional provincial city sought to embrace modern industry with energy and in a manner that bode well for the future. An indication of the latter, in view of the troubles emerging in São Paulo, could be seen in Curitiba's efforts from the outset, to attract non-polluting industries. This, in particular, distinguished it from the other large industrial centers.

Second, while the main thrust was the effort to interest investments from abroad and from elsewhere in Brazil, CIC provided ample space for local industries that sought to expand and to do so without most of the restrictions that applied in the often inner city sites in which so many of them were then located. Although the same space might be found elsewhere in the Curitiba Metropolitan Area and at lower prices than in CIC, those areas did not offer infrastructure that was as suitable. For at least one local enterprise, a firm that was growing rapidly and was soon to become a national leader in its field, the establishment of CIC and the arrival of many prominent firms would provide it with new customers to supply. This incentive led INEPAR to refrain from a projected move to Minas Gerais.

A third incentive, in the decade of the 1970s at least, was that given the infrastructure provided, the price of the CIC industrial sites clearly was subsidized. While the cost of the land usually was a small part of the overall expenditure and probably was rarely a really decisive factor, it is notable that some purchasers did not build on part of the terrain they purchased for up to ten years.

Fourth, various forms of government assistance were available. The Federal Government had a special fund for municipal development, linked to the Presidency, but that was available to all of the cities of the country in the 1970s and early 1980s, and it is claimed that Belo Horizonte was more successful in tapping those funds. At the state level, there were several incentives. There were tax exemptions and postponements, as well as arrangements for provisional stock purchases with allowances for subsequent company buy-backs. Both were substantially reduced by the 1980s as Curitiba became better known as an industrial center (and as Brazil encountered major financial and economic problems). Equally important was the availability of financing from BADEP, and, in those years, that meant subsidized financing because the BADEP loan balances outstanding were not readjusted to reflect inflation at that time. Materials are not available to put a dollar value on all of this, and it is unlikely that the offers made to enterprises exceeded those available from Minas Gerais, long involved in such promotion, but the amount of subsidy undoubtedly was a factor in decision making in the 1970s. Even so, then BADEP head Richbieter cautioned prospective investors that the incentives were likely to come to an end so enterprises were going to have to be viable in order to survive.

Finally, an incentive often mentioned for the 1970s and still cited, is that labor costs were lower in Curitiba than in most industrial centers, perhaps 40 percent lower than in São Paulo at that time (for engineers and skilled labor as well as for unskilled personnel). Moreover, labor unions, which were local, were less aggressive than in São Paulo. Indeed, to the extent that it was necessary to recruit skilled laborers from elsewhere, efforts were directed first to Joinville and Blumenau in Santa Catarina, Caxias do Sul and

Porto Alegre in Rio Grande do Sul, and Belo Horizonte in Minas Gerais. Real wages probably were of the same order in Porto Alegre as in São Paulo so that what was at issue in that case was the nature of labor-management relations as much as real cost differences.

Constructed in 1973-74, the Industrial City of Curitiba was formally inaugurated March 4, 1975. As early as 1973, there were commitments from three local enterprises (in textiles, chemicals and plastics), Ford New Holland (agricultural equipment), Siemens/Equitel and Philip Morris as well as the first of what was to be a group of Japanese companies. Negotiations were underway with Volvo, Bosch, Nippondenso and others, and 14 enterprises followed in 1974, 20 in 1975, with another 125 by the end of 1982. Although some companies utilized local raw materials, particularly at the outset and then again in the early 1980s when CIC became independent and sought sales of smaller lots, industry in CIC involved less reliance on backward linkages than in Minas Gerais or Santa Catarina, and less than had been the case in Paraná past. Moreover, at first many parts and components were purchased from firms in São Paulo and elsewhere but over time, Inepar, Volvo and a number of other CIC enterprises made special efforts to develop local suppliers, the lack of which had inhibited the relocation of some other companies to the city. Metalworking products, electrical and transportation equipment and tobacco products began to show new strength in the industrial output of Paraná. Even in such traditional activities as woodworking, paper and chemicals, there were important shifts in the composition of products towards those of higher value added. Between 1970 and 1982, the share of Paraná in Brazil's industrial output more than doubled, from just under 3 to more than 6 percent, with most of the increase emanating from enterprises in CIC. Suddenly, Paraná's share of Brazilian industry was nearly as great as in the more traditional manufacturing center of Porto Alegre, and not far below that of Minas Gerais. Manufacturing industry, with a value added only two-thirds that of Paraná's agricultural and grazing sector in 1970, came to have a value added more than 50 percent larger only a decade later. All of the new industrial investment was from the private sector while in Minas Gerais, two-thirds was contributed by the state government in the 1970s.

Despite the tax exemptions and postponements granted to many new investors, Curitiba's share of the value-added tax paid in the State of Paraná, doubled between 1970 and 1982. The success of the new industrial city seemed well underway, aided in part by close cooperation between leaders from the private and public sectors in formal and informal associations.

Although this was acknowledged as a factor in the favorable evolution of CIC, it has also been characterized as a corporative relationship of interest groups by some of those who viewed the new developments in Curitiba with mixed feelings.[1] Critical positions are considered further in the chapter that follows. In any event, what transpired in Curitiba provides a strong exception to the comment of two American economists who, in reviewing urban planning experiences, concluded that "business-oriented infrastructure investments, have by and large, failed to appear." (Beesley and Kemp, in Mills 1987: 1046).

---

[1]   In his account of industrialization in Belo Horizonte, Eakin observes, "A strongly corporatist ethos characterized the mentality of the business elite in Belo Horizonte, indeed, in all Brazil." Eakin 2001: 46.

5

Reconsidering the Nature of the City's Development: 1983-1988 and Beyond

The same approach to Curitiba's socioeconomic development continued during three consecutive municipal administrations—from 1971 through 1982. Moreover, IPPUC, the linchpin of that transformation, was initiated in 1965-66 and persevered, even if on a back burner during the years before 1971, providing an important part of the critical preparatory work for what followed. By 1971, IPPUC had become the principal source for basic development proposals and the analysis of issues in addition to providing many of the practical solutions to problems. Objections to the nature of the city's new evolution were voiced from the outset, of course, they began to increase in 1982-83 with the onset of the Latin American Debt Crisis and recession in Brazil, and they were accentuated by an agricultural crisis in Paraná in 1983-84. Government funding for major urban projects became scarcer, Brazilian companies became less interested in investing and in considering relocations to Curitiba, and the inflow of new investment from abroad declined sharply. In 1982, the newly elected state governor, representing a political party opposed to Jaime Lerner, designated Maurício Fruet to be Mayor of Curitiba. Fruet was an individual with doubts about the recent course of the city's evolution. Economic recovery in Paraná was still lagging in 1986, the first year of municipal elections in more than two decades, and Roberto Requião, a bitter foe of Jaime Lerner and Curitiba's altered course, defeated Lerner in his initial bid for a third period as the city's mayor.

59

Those in power in Curitiba during the period 1983-1988 (and in the statehouse from 1983-1994) expressed a growing number of concerns. First, they believed that too much attention had been given to downtown Curitiba and the immediately adjacent areas, and that much more needed to be done in the outlying neighborhoods. Second, the new administrations felt that the city's economic boom had largely by-passed lower income groups and that more attention needed to be devoted to them. In particular, they believed that more should be done to alleviate the condition of the rapidly emerging slums, that there should be substantial additions to infrastructure in those neighborhoods—areas which the previous administrations had hoped would not become major home sites because they lie in flood plains. Those areas were experiencing rapid population growth and the numbers estimated to be living in slums increased by approximately two-thirds between 1974 and 1978, amounting to 4 percent of the city's population. Third, doubts were expressed about CIC, particularly by opposition political groups but also by representatives of traditional Curitiba some of whom endorsed the efforts of the Lerner Group to revive the city, as the demand for industrial tracts slowed during the mid-1980s. This was one reason behind the new administrations' acquiescence to the invasions of the public land there and in the nearby, relatively unused and particularly flood-prone private land in the southern part of the city. Fourth, interest was manifested in recharting the nature of Curitiba's development, or, in any event, in filling in what were perceived as gaps. Fruet, the first of the two opposition mayors submitted an updated and revised set of Guidelines for the city, though this came at the close of his administration and was not given much attention by his successor, Roberto Requião. In addition, there was an attempt, particularly by Requião, to discredit the activities of Jaime Lerner and his associates.

By the late 1990s, the number of concerns had increased, and while some of these reflected developments yet to be outlined, it is useful to consider all of them together. (Much of what follows is taken from Samek 1996 and Sánchez Garcia 1996.)

First, although more had been done to establish neighborhood centers by the mid-1990s, objections still were voiced about an overemphasis on downtown and on what critics termed the monument-like park sites, which though not in the heart of the city, were most easily accessible to those with autos. It was pointed out that per capita income levels and infrastructure deficiencies varied widely from neighborhood to neighborhood.

Second, somewhat related, critics maintained that it was necessary to emphasize projects that gave special attention to lower income groups. How

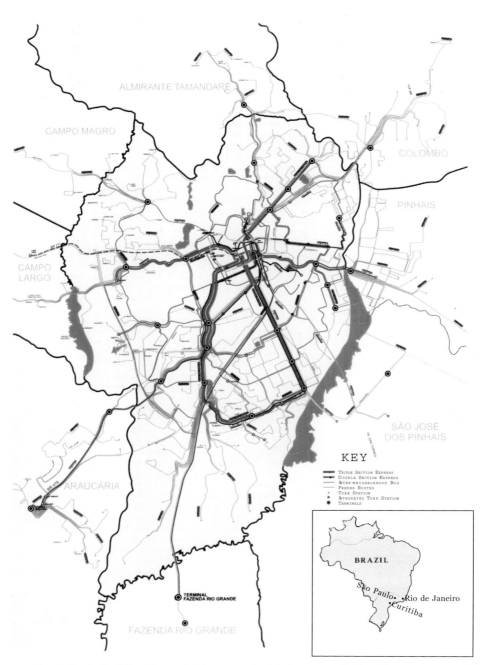

KEY

TRIPLE SECTION EXPRESS
DOUBLE SECTION EXPRESS
INTER-NEIGHBORHOOD BUS
FEEDER ROUTES
TUBE STATION
INTEGRATED TUBE STATION
TERMINALS

1. *Curitiba's Public Transit System (with insert of Brazil).* Courtesy of
   IPPUC.

2. *Triple Section Bus on one of the dedicated (exclusive) bus lanes:* Curitiba Secretariat of Social Communication (MSSC)

3. *The traditional Main Street after the initiation of the pedestrian mall: 15th of November Street (with fountain)*: MSSC

4. *The University of the Free Environment (former abandoned quarry)*: MSSC

5. *The University of the Free Environment (former abandoned quarry):*
MSSC

6. *The traditional Main Street pedestrian mall: 15ᵗʰ of November Street:* MSSC

7. *The Botanic Garden (former garbage dump):* MSSC

8. *Barigui Park:* MSSC

9. *Barigui Park:* MSSC

10.Bike Path: MSSC

11. Sunday fair (two blocks from fair center of Garibaldi Square):
Collection of Charles Wright

12. *Buses, downtown bus stop with dual glass and steel passenger tubes:* MSSC

13. *Passengers entering and exiting at tubular bus loading point:* Wright Collection

14. Bus with platforms extended to tubular passenger loading point:
Wright Collection

15. Passengers loading at a bus terminal: Wright Collection

16. Wheelchair ascending to passenger tube platform: Wright Collection

17. Curitiba Industrial City (now Curitiba Development Company): MSSC

*18. 24 Hour Street:*MSSC

19. *Traditional Paraná pine tree:* MSSC

could it be that in a metropolitan area so characterized by springs and river basins that the residents of some areas were subject to water rationing on occasion? (This was most serious in areas outside the city limits, it should be noted.) Only 60 percent of city residents had sewer connections at the end of the 1980s, and only a quarter of human waste was chemically treated. The percentages were much lower in the generally poorer adjoining communities, in some of which there were no sewer connections at all. Flood control remained a problem in the newly occupied regions of Curitiba. Infant mortality was better than the average for Brazil but not as low as in several other cities. Hospitals were readily available in the wealthier parts of the city, but there was a shortage of hospital beds in the qualified public hospitals and clinics that serviced lower income areas. It was claimed that the rate of accidents in the workplace was high and that transit accidents with fatal injuries were among the highest in Brazil despite the highly acclaimed public transportation system that reduced reliance on private vehicles. Available nurseries could handle only about a fifth of the young children in the city, and though a UNICEF study ranked Curitiba second among the nation's state capitals in infant survival rates, it claimed that the quality of life for children was only 74th among the 181 major communities (which does not seem even remotely plausible). A study by IPARDES reported that 89,000 minors, ages 10-17, participated in the workforce, nearly half for 40 hours a week or more, and that 80 percent of them had not completed primary school. Both the state and municipal school systems in Curitiba were criticized—for the quality of what they offered, for their lack of attention to computer literacy and because of the high drop-out rate. This was contrasted with the private schools where most high income and many middle income families sent their children.

While the growing rate of unemployment was recognized to be a problem primarily for national policy, it was claimed that the city was not taking enough measures to help, as, for example, by establishing an Employment Bank. The city was criticized for having delayed so long before issuing building permits for the southern part of the city and before providing low interest rate loans to the working poor to purchase lots on which to build simple homes. It was noted that the quality of the air in some neighborhoods was poor, though it was acknowledged that it was especially bad only near the refinery located in the neighboring city of Araucária. The cultural incentives program was characterized as too elitist. Finally, official reports of IPPUC were cited indicating that approximately 100,000 (about 7 percent of the city's population) lived in clandestine settlements without basic urban infrastructure and another 100,000 to 200,000 resided in marginal areas with only minimal infrastructure. While these proportions are lower than in other large cities of Brazil, they might not be that much lower for the Curitiba Metropolitan Region as a whole. Living conditions in these slum areas are worse than in any I am aware of in the United States, but not as bad as in many slums in other Brazilian cities.

Third, there were a few complaints concerning the Industrial City of Curitiba (as of 1992, the Development Company of Curitiba) that came from industrialists who were on balance quite favorable to Curitiba's new direction. With the surge of new industrial investments beginning in the late 1980s, the criticism of CIC eased, but consistent with the comments above, maintenance of the area's infrastructure had been allowed to decline somewhat during the years 1983-88.

Fourth, the 1985 Municipal Plan for Urban Development: Although several points raised in the Guidelines commissioned by Mayor Fruet coincided with those mentioned elsewhere in this chapter, particularly those stressing the need for more emphasis on the social and less on the technical aspects of development, Fruet's attempt to provide a new set of guidelines for the city was largely ignored, both by those opposed to Lerner who succeeded him and those of the Lerner Group who followed in the period beginning 1989.

Fifth, the Marketing of Curitiba as a city with an outstanding Quality of Life, the Ecological Capital, One of the Three Most Livable Cities in the World, etc. has been treated with derision and contempt by political opponents and many in the intellectual community. In part, this has to do with the amounts spent on publicity—far more than in the similar size to somewhat larger cities of Porto Alegre and Belo Horizonte. Moreover, the Marketing of Curitiba appears to have contributed to the resurgence of a migration of people to Curitiba metropolitan area in the 1990s, most of whom lacked the education or skills required in the increasingly technical types of manufacturing and service activities that the city was attracting. Publicity expenditures may have set some sort of record during the 1995 municipal elections when the Administration flooded television with advertisements of its activities, paid for from public funds. The main complaints about this came from the Workers Party (PT), a political party which until recently, had been given little chance of winning at the city-or statewide level. The centrist opposition groups, which had gained power periodically, have had much less to say about this type of public expenditure. As important as this questionable funding of political advertising is in principle, the strongest objection derives from the alternative uses to which the funds could be put, and the degree to which the quality of life without such expenditures, while better than in the communities from which the poorest have come, nonetheless, leaves something to be desired. (Surveys have shown, though, that even in the slums of Curitiba, very few consider returning to the areas from which they came.)

The sixth concern relates to certain socioeconomic data. Information from several sources reveals that violent crime has been increasing in Curitiba, and the rate of homicides, while much lower than in Rio or São Paulo, is now at the level of Salvador and New York—much higher than in several European and Japanese cities. One report alleges that 8 percent of those in Metropolitan Curitiba are homeless (most presumably outside the Curitiba city limits). Two studies based on 1991 census data concluded that Curitiba ranked only fourth among Brazilian cities in terms of its quality of life. Aside from the subjectivity necessarily involved in such rankings (two of the first three cities differed in the two studies, for example), one of the communities that ranked higher appears to have a policy of meeting poorly dressed arrivals at the bus station, and if they are jobseekers, of escorting them to a bus returning to the city from which they came, providing them with the ticket necessary for the trip. More to the point perhaps, a study undertaken by IPPUC but apparently never made public, indicates that in 1995, while average living standards had risen appreciably, there were thirteen neighborhoods in the city that lacked certain basic urban infrastructure. A report prepared by IPARDES concluded that 19-29 percent of the city's population found themselves in what was judged to be a precarious position—this in a city with a somewhat smaller proportion of those in the lowest income brackets than the other large cities of the country. Contributing to the IPARDES conclusion is the cost of living in Curitiba, among the lowest of large cities in Brazil in the 1970s and 1980s, but higher than most by the mid-to-late 1990s. (To provide a more up-to-date perspective, however, as noted in the Introduction, a United Nations report prepared in the late 1990s concluded that Curitiba was the Brazilian state capital with the highest living standards and the lowest number of people living in poverty.)

Finally, several complaints had been raised over the years concerning municipal administration. The opposition had clamored for the decentralization of more administrative activities, and when in power, took steps in that direction. Somewhat related to that, has been the insistence on a more participatory governing process (more along the lines initiated in the 1990s in Porto Alegre), with the Lerner Group accused of employing an excessively top-down approach. In addition, there have been complaints that too many agencies deal with the same subject matter. As examples, several separate municipal entities have been involved at times in implementing the *Guidelines* and during a few years during the 1990s, two separate municipal agencies were active in promoting industrial development (in addition to CIC). Further, noting the relatively low percentage of salaries and wages to total expenditures in the administrations of the Lerner Group (50 percent), the opposition parties have criticized what they characterized as the overemphasis on physical investment (as compared to investment in human resources and expenditures on social services), the low salaries of most municipal employees (which discourage higher productivity, they have contended), and the city's extensive use of outsourcing, allegedly to favored enterprises (which are said to earn substantial incomes but to pay particularly low wages to their employees). Among the other major complaints has been the lack, for the most part, of a truly independent City Council—though it is acknowledged that the City Council blocked approval of the light rail system in 1989. The latter, initially a project favored by the mayor, would have been much more expensive than the alternative selected (described in the following chapter).

There is merit in some of these complaints, and, as is indicated in the next chapter, the Lerner Group has taken many of them into account and has modified a number of its earlier orientations. While critics continue to provide valuable critiques and to set forth proposals to meliorate some of the city's most serious problems, it is noteworthy that opposition municipal administrations failed to reverse the growth of slums when they were in power. Moreover, neither those political parties nor others of a more radical orientation have been able to devise plans for Curitiba's future that have competed very effectively with the visions of the Lerner Group. Though the doubters are now more numerous than before, Jaime Lerner and his associates triumphed easily in three of the last four municipal elections (winning in the fourth as well) and in two of the last three contests for governor. Indeed, in the Year 2000 campaign for mayor, the opposition party that came closest to defeating the defeating the incumbents, the Workers Party, was less critical than the traditional centrist opposition of what had been accomplished in Curitiba to date, emphasizing instead, differences in their approach for the period ahead. More on Curitiba politics in Appendix B.

6

Ecological Aspirations and Increased International Recognition

The implementation of Curitiba's 1966 *Guidelines* had been advanced substantially by the end of the Second Lerner Administration in 1982, and several matters that had not been given much attention in those *Guidelines* had received greater emphasis in the mid-1980s from the administrations of the centrist opposition. What then, would the Lerner Group seek to do as it returned to power in late 1988 and in the years thereafter?

One objective, of course, would be to continue addressing those elements of the *Guidelines* that still required more attention or that were in need of modification. This would include whatever measures might be necessary to assure the success of the city's vast industrial park—a liberal rendering of the separate industrial district called for in the *Guidelines*. A second objective would be to build upon some of the measures that the opposition had emphasized in the 1980s, providing more assistance to those who had not been among the major beneficiaries of the increases in per capita income registered since 1970. A third objective related to the introduction of new development visions that would add further to the quality of life and address the globally increasing concern about ecology. All of this may have overlapped with another objective—to advance the possibility that Jaime Lerner, probably Brazil's best-known mayor, would run for president. Whether or not Lerner himself sought to be President of Brazil, he was encouraged to run for Governor of Paraná in part as a stepping stone. In late 1995, polls indicated that then Governor Lerner had an approval rating of 83%, and many newspaper articles claimed that his party was considering a Lerner candidacy in place of its perennial standard bearer, the controversial Leonel Brizola.[1]

To begin, consider two important changes that were taking place.

The mid-1980s were years of reduced rates of economic growth, but, nonetheless, significant evolution in the State of Paraná. The agricultural sector declined further in relative importance, but the productivity and competitivity of many products increased, aided by added mechanization, the technical assistance of TECPAR and other institutes, and new signs of entrepreneurship, particularly in several cooperatives. Industrial production, which had reached 6 percent of Brazilian output in 1980, declined and then stagnated at about 4.5 percent during most of the decade (while in neighboring Santa Catarina, manufacturing's share of national manufacturing rose sharply, from 3 to 4.8 percent). The composition of the industrial sector continued to change, with woodworking, textile and foodstuffs declining further in relative terms, while major gains were registered in the shares of electrical and transportation products, tobacco, chemicals, and metalworking. Shifts were pronounced within the branches of industry as well. The competitiveness of various products was facilitated by the growing importance of multinational enterprises and the increasing contribution of the technical training institutions— the two principal universities, CEFET (which introduced the first specialized course in Brazil on technological innovation), the State Polytechnic Institute, TECPAR, the Electronics Laboratory, the Industrial Technology Center, the Brazilian Institute of Quality and Productivity, the Paraná Technological Integration Center, and in the 1990s, the Software Park of the Industrial City.

In addition, the population of the State of Paraná was becoming increasingly concentrated in Curitiba and environs; the Metropolitan Curitiba Region accounted for somewhat under 12 percent of the State total in 1970 but nearly double that percentage by 1990. National perception of what was taking place in Curitiba may have exceeded even the impressive reality. In 1972, only a year after he entered into office, Brazilian journalists had termed Jaime Lerner the best mayor in the nation. By the early 1990s that type of accolade appeared in prominent newspapers all over the world. Curitiba's good name led to special awards in 1990 from the United Nations Program on the Environment and the International Institute for the Conservation of Energy. In 1992, just before the Rio Conference on the Environment and Development, Curitiba was the site of a World Urban Forum. Even more prominent distinctions followed in the mid-1990s as the city gained fame for its livability and ecological awareness.[2] In 1995, Curitiba was selected to host the United Nations' Habitat I, and the following year, one of Curitiba's innovative new buses was displayed at the transportation exhibit in Habitat II, held in Istanbul, Turkey.

The essence of what the Lerner Group believed they were doing—certainly the way they sought to be perceived—emerges from remarks made by Jaime Lerner in 1992 and 1993, as he was turning the administration of the city over to close colleagues.

> The environmentally correct city should give preeminence to collective over individual transport, economizing fuel and reducing the need for investments in various public works. The environmentally correct city avoids forced industrialization, rejects polluting industries—and obliges government and producers to invest in clean technology. The environmentally correct city intervenes to avoid the segregation of urban functions and social classes. The integration of urban functions helps the city to economize or maximize, because it reduces the number of dislocations. Just as the city ought to be environmentally correct, so too, it should become socially correct. The first step is to invest in children, opening the paths of equality for those who are most in need, and in so doing, reducing the impact of poverty. A socially correct city should invest to the maximum in works that deal with the quality of life, in order to improve the city and create employment. It should optimize collective transport, which in addition to reducing the number of automobiles in the streets, democratizes the access to urban accoutrements. The socially correct city should democratize leisure, increasing the extent of green areas, parks, bicycle paths, and all of the meeting places of its inhabitants. (Lerner 1992, cited in Menezes 1996: 149. Translation by the author of this manuscript, authorized by Jaime Lerner.)

In 1993, in an interview, Lerner added:

> What exists in Curitiba is a strategic vision. What is a strategic vision? I would say that it is a balance between the necessities that the populace presses for every day and the potential that those responsible for the city (the mayors, city councilmen, and leaders) have the obligation to aim for…. [I]f one doesn't have a strategic vision, one doesn't undertake changes….[I]f one concentrates only on the daily problems of the mass of the people (employment and problems of transportation and health), one strays from what is truly sought, deep-down . For this reason it is necessary to attempt to address both sets of

concerns. This day-to-day balance is necessary in all professional activities. If one doesn't take the time for matters of a greater global vision as well as for the day-to-day concerns, one ends up losing. It is necessary to attend to what is important and to what is fundamental at the same time. And while everything is important, some things are fundamental. (Interview with Lerner, 1993, cited in Menezes 1996, 151. Free translation authorized by Governor Lerner.)

The principal spheres of action of the Lerner Group from 1989 through 1998 fell under the following headings: public transportation; regulation of land use; advancement of neighborhood civic centers; expansion of public parks and forests; promotion of a unique urban landscape; attention to social concerns; increased attention to the area outside the city limits—planning in terms of the Metropolitan Curitiba Region; promotion of private enterprise; and attention to ecological concerns and new visions.

Curitiba's efforts in the area of public transportation began the urban restructuring and are those for which the city is best known so perhaps that discussion can be left to last. Many of the considerations taken into account in regulating land use were related to decisions concerning traffic routes and public transportation, however. The guidelines for land use proposals in Curitiba emerged from eleven considerations reflecting location and past land use. Key has been location in one of the following: a) the traditional center of the city; b) a "structural" sector (location along one of the five main transportation axes proceeding out from center city); c) the historic zone; d) a connecting road zone (the five axes that link the Industrial City with one of the principal traffic arteries of the city); e) collecting road sectors; f) river basins; g) the Santa Felicidade neighborhood, h) the Industrial City; i) areas of higher education; j) green areas (parks and forest preserves); and k) military areas. Approximately six dozen laws have defined the physical boundaries of these areas and specified the types of structures that can be built and activities that can be undertaken in each category of land. All this regulation provides for orderliness but also reflects a measure of arbitrariness. It is urban planning that is a compromise between a particular vision of what is seen as architecturally desirable and what strikes those in power as politically viable, subject to some economic constraints. That is remote from any optimization process as economists would define one, and yet this is one of the world's most successful cases of urban planning.

The reality of mushrooming settlements in the flood-prone southern sector pushed the city to reconsider the categories assigned to those areas, legalize the residence of many individuals in what had been previously been categorized as marginal areas to be left largely idle, and even open up sections of those lands for building permits (including for owner construction).[3] The population explosion in these areas overwhelmed the approach of the late 1970s of attempting to resolve problems by relocating slum dwellers from ecologically unsound areas to others, and placing them in specially constructed public housing. The shift led, in turn, to the provision of basic urban infrastructure where it had been hoped that there would be none— though much less than that which Carlos Arthur Kruger Passos, the economist who headed up IPARDES in the opposition Administrations of the late 1980s had recommended.

Little was done to truly decentralize decision making, though neighborhood interaction sessions with representatives of IPPUC were set up beginning 1978. The promotion of neighborhood civic centers was accorded more attention after the mid-80s, first in the opposition Administrations and then, in then, in the early-to-mid-90s, in the Municipal Administration of Lerner colleague, Rafael Greca. In particular, special conglomerations of health stations, libraries, gymnasiums, environmental information centers, etc. were set up at a number of the transportation terminals. In addition, 20 "lighthouses of knowledge," small libraries in the shape of colorful lighthouses were constructed, with 30 more planned. The proliferation of these eye-catching structures with only a small number of books (instead of more substantial additions to the main public library) was criticized by some, but did bring at least rudimentary libraries to many of those in outlying areas of the municipality who did not have the time or for other reasons did not get to the principal facility, downtown. Moreover, by the late 1990s these lighthouses of knowledge also provided access to the internet.

The extraordinary expansion of public parks and forests in a city whose population was tripling must stand out as one of the centerpieces of the Lerner Group undertakings. Curitiba, which had only a single significant park in 1970, now has more than two dozen, one, a splendid botanic garden and museum established at a site which up to that time, had served as a garbage dump. Public green space has increased by twenty-fold (even a good deal more by some accounts). These parks (many with artifacts honoring particular ethnic groups of the city's population) and their connecting bicycle paths provided a major increase in outdoor leisure opportunities for all social classes; they also have proved an effective means of dealing with the river runoffs that have so plagued Curitiba, as noted. The first of these new parks was inaugurated in 1972, but the largest additions to the system were established in the 1990s.

A major objective of the Lerner Group has always been the promotion of a unique urban landscape. The most singular aspect of this, the extended pedestrian mall in the city's principal commercial street, has already been discussed. Also early on, a long-abandoned gunpowder storage facility was transformed into a theater, and other buildings (even factories) have been recycled to become a Center of Creativity, a Center of Graphic Arts and Music Education, a Conservatory of Popular Brazilian Music, a center of historical documents of the city, the first municipal museum in the country, a center city nursery, etc. Most of this was coordinated by a municipal entity, the Cultural Foundation of Curitiba. A jewel in the downtown area, but one that predates the Lerner Administrations, is the Guairá Theater, the principal center for musical and theatrical events that offers special low-fee concerts on Sunday morning as well as regular evening performances. The singular "24 Hour Street," established in the 1990s, is a place to eat and shop, night and day (photograph 18). That now famous alleyway has been criticized by some in the center-left opposition as an example of the use of resources for "show" instead of for socially urgent needs, but the overall impact is certainly inviting. Downtown Curitiba is a place to come to and to enjoy.

Nor does the unique urban landscape end there. Further out is the Free University of the Environment with its eye-catching, rustic winding staircase and conference room peering out over a man-made lake in which swans cavort about. There is also the Wire Opera House, a partially enclosed structure seating 3,000 and the adjoining open space for public spectacles that can accommodate 50,000. Still further out, the landscape is much as it always was—except, of course, for those areas with parks. The impact of all of this and of all of the additions to green space is striking, but wait. Does all this reflect the implementation of Curitiba's famous "Master Plan?" Does it reflect the sort of urban planning that is supposed to have characterized Curitiba? Is it possible to find support for that in the reasoning processes of IPPUC? (Alas, IPPUC's deliberations have not been open, records of those decision making process are not available to the public, and there may not be any permanent record of the nature of those deliberations. There are indications that what transpired involved a good deal of "incrementalism," along with some use of judgmental heuristics—Rules of Thumb—with IPPUC developing an increasing ability to gauge the biases and improve the Rules of Thumb.) How does one weigh the value of the parks, which also serve as protective measure against flooding and distinctive urban landscape, against the complaints of under investment in the social sector—even in strictly economic terms? The level of per capita income in Curitiba increased dramatically, in absolute terms and relative to other cities. So, too, did the access of the populace to civic amenities.

There has always been a certain attention to social concerns, but admittedly that was not the principal focus of the Master Plan or the initial implementation of that Plan. Jaime Lerner and his group began as visionaries who sought to restructure the face of Curitiba so as to improve the city's livability and also meet the challenges of the 1960s and 1970s by providing a new potential for growth. Consider, too, that from the outset, Curitiba had a lower percentage of the very poor than the other major Brazilian cities.

Among the first efforts in what might be considered the social area were those in the field of education. The Lerner Group added to the number of municipal schools at a rate more rapid than population growth, but perhaps their most notable contribution was to emphasize the character and quality of human resources. One example was the establishment of schools offering the "international baccalaureate." These were to provide a particularly strong education for the children of the executives and middle managers of the anticipated new industries (although most of those children would likely attend private schools). The general improvement of the city's educational offerings coupled with the incentive of increasing opportunities for employment that depended upon greater educational achievement led to a rise in literacy rates which reached 94 percent by the mid-1990s (compared to the nationwide figure of little more than 80%). This despite the continuing arrival of hundreds of thousands with very limited educational preparation.

The impressive increase in health care centers and in nurseries of the mid-1980s continued in the Lerner Group Administrations that followed. Both nearly doubled in numbers, though even at that, nurseries were available for only about a third of the children under six years of age (perhaps half of those whose parents might have sought such facilities). The municipal low-cost centers for the supply of basic foodstuffs continued, though at a somewhat reduced level. What seems extraordinarily impressive at first glance but is particularly difficult to evaluate, is the impact of the individual items on the long list of activities of the city's Social Action Foundation. The Foundation dealt with health care, education, housing, food supply, the environment, and childcare. It ran schools that provided training for 30,000 teenagers and young adults in 60 trades. Among its activities was a much publicized but very small Trades Village Program that rehabilitated small fragile homes into colorful structures that served as workshops on the first floor and living quarters on the second. And the Foundation coordinated

"All Clean," temporary street cleaning jobs for the unemployed. (Downtown Curitiba probably has the cleanest center city of any of the large metropolises in the country.) The Foundation's other programs included the following:

- A job search office, which in 1997, in the Administration of Cassio Taniguchi,was expanded into an "Employment Line" program. A $100 million program ($75 million from the National Development Bank for infrastructure), the project is developing a series of community sheds along a newly constructed 20 mile avenue adjacent to the transmission lines of COPEL, running through five low income neighborhoods from the eastern to the southern parts of the city. These will serve as artisan training and recruitment centers and aim to create 30,000-50,000 new jobs (some estimates are a good deal higher)).
- Citizen-Cart, a waste paper collection program;
- Justice and Citizenship, a community service program for petty offenders;
- SOS—Street educators for the down and out;
- Social Guidance Center, with emergency transportation tokens, food and hospital care;
- A Senior Citizen Program;
- Grandmother's Voucher, offering kits of food and health products to men and women over 65 with income below the minimum wage;
- An Emergency Services Center for street people with 64 beds;
- Solidarity Farm; a modified version of a program first proposed in 1982 that aimed at those addicted to alcohol and drugs;
- A Family Relocation Program;
- Organizational assistance for low income communities;
- Supper Line, a soup kitchen;
- A bootblack apprenticeship program;
- A junk hotline;
- A social resources integration program;
- Moving assistance for families with incomes below the level of "two minimum wages;"
- Martha's Shelter, for battered women and a hotline for abandoned or abused women and older citizens;
- An Expectant Mother's Program; and
- Neighborhood (community) homes.

In addition there was a public sector/private sector Pro-Citizenship Institute with a variety of programs.

Yet visits to the *favelas* that now contain approximately 7 percent of the city's population leave the impression that there are those among the most needy who are unaware of or unable to take advantage of most of those programs. Even so, few consider returning to the communities from which they have come. It is not clear to what extent the increasing social emphasis of the Lerner Group has been due to the increasing importance of these matters (certainly a factor), the increasing recognition of them as fairness considerations—legitimization considerations[4]—by a group previously more enmeshed in architectural designs, etc., or the political expediency of modifying goals in the light of public pressure (perhaps one of the keys to the successful implementation that was critical for the success of Curitiba's *Master Plan* from the very outset). Even if the last of the three was the most important, the merits of what was done should receive as much weight as the motivations involved (which, in any event, might have represented in part an effort at social coordination). Surely the world abounds with municipal reformers who meant well but were not able to achieve much of what they sought and did not leave their cities better off.

References to Curitiba as the Ecological Capital of Brazil are recent, but ecological concerns date back more than half a century. The Agache Plan of the early 1940s urged that building permits not be granted for river basin areas. Later, in the mid-1950s, ordinances were approved setting forth requirements for replanting trees and regulating forest preservation, mineral extraction and garbage disposal. The *Master Plan* prepared in 1966 also touched on some of these matters.

In the 1970s, environmental concerns contributed to the decision to develop large parks with lakes that would collect river runoffs, and to more stringent requirements concerning tree replacement. In 1974 alone, the city government planted 60,000 trees. This was undertaken in part in conjunction with flood control programs, as was the development of linear parks—environmental corridors—along waterways and highways. As of the early 1990s, more than 200,000 trees had been planted along 700 miles of roads. Throughout the '70s and '80s more large parks with flood collection areas were created, increasingly in the most vulnerable southern and eastern parts of the city. Efforts to reduce pollution in the headwaters of the Belem River date to 1980-82 and a metropolitan region plan for the protection of the Iguaçu River, to 1983. The Fruet Administration (1983-85) made special efforts to protect the areas that served as the sources for Curitiba's rivers, and with the increasing evidence of garbage dumps, passed a law requiring that owners clear their land of garbage or pay the city for having it done. (Since 1984 the city has contracted garbage collection to a private company.)

A high level municipal office on the environment was established under Mayor Requião (1986-88) and regulations followed requiring the monitoring of water pollution, the preservation of green areas, the planting of trees adjacent to buildings, further controls on garbage (including that of the Industrial City), and the granting of property tax allowances for land with a certain level of green coverage. (The last of those subsequently became a statewide law.) Publicity campaigns concerning the environment were initiated and during the third administration of Jaime Lerner these were intensified and coordinated with educational programs in the schools and parks. The position of Secretary of Environmental Health was established in 1991 with an ambitious agenda and charged with the construction of a new solid waste disposal site. That same year marked the opening of the Free University of the Environment, which, like the Wire Opera House, was built on the remains of an abandoned quarry.

In 1992 separate septic tanks for hospital waste were established. The famous "Garbage that Isn't Garbage" campaign for the separation of the various types of waste was inaugurated in 1989. The city estimates that as many as 70 percent of Curitiba's households participate in this program, with garbage separated, picked up, and ultimately recycled. This author's admittedly casual observation in 1995, 1997 and 1998 suggests that the recycling probably does not affect an especially large part of the Curitiba's garbage, but what is being done certainly surpasses that of most and perhaps all other cities in Latin America. There also are Garbage Purchase and Green Exchange programs whereby those who live in areas that are inaccessible to large trucks can leave their garbage at established points, and receive, in exchange, certain basic foodstuffs, transportation tokens and toys. This leads to the collection of more of the city's trash, contributing to sanitation objectives. The program is said to have involved an annual average of about 10,000 families between 1989 and 1992, and the number may be somewhat larger at present. Such activities help explain the substantial reduction in infant mortality that was recorded between the early and mid-1990s. All of these undertakings seem to have made a contribution, whether or not they justified the full extent of the claims made for the city as an ecological showplace. There does not seem to have been any overall plan for ecological advancement and I have not been able to uncover either ex-ante or ex post cost-benefit analyses for these ecological projects. Each was promoted because it struck key officials as making good sense—as responding to some useful Rule of Thumb—and the various programs certainly have added to the quality of life in Curitiba and to the pride of many in the city. Whether the projects really were among the best (and the best sequenced) is not something that would be easy to assess—though they do seem better (and better sequenced) than in the other major cities of the country.

Jaime Lerner's own synthesis of the accomplishments of his third administration can be found in endnote 1 to this chapter. Beyond that, he offers the following observations:

> No Master Plan, no government plan will succeed without a vision of solidarity. Everyone talks about Curitiba's Master Plan, Curitiba's urban planning, etc. Most important, I think, is that we always had in mind that humanizing Curitiba was essential.
>
> And that can be easily noticed in every aspect of Curitiba. Its public transportation, for example, is above all, a gesture of solidarity. In addition to ensuring increasing comfort, safety and efficiency to the mass transportation system, a social fare was created. For the first time, a Brazilian city adopted a single fare, in which shorter trips subsidize longer ones (rendering the fare cheaper to those living in the outskirts, typically the poorest). This is pure income distribution. A good transportation system is a guarantee of fewer cars in the streets. And every first grade student knows that this represents better quality of air in the city. In the beginning of the seventies, Curitiba had only 0.5 square meters of green space per inhabitant. Today, this figure is 52 square meters of green space per inhabitant, one of the highest rates in the world. Does this contribute to a better quality of air in the city? I guess common sense says it does. We never had a major plan of becoming the ecological capital of the world. We just went on doing things we were sure would be good for the environment and for our population. That was our measure. Lerner 2003.

There have been several examples of learning from experience that have reoriented efforts to continue the industrial expansion of Curitiba. In the early 1980s, when CIC was separated from URBS, even before the downturn in the Brazilian economy, financial pressures led to a decision to rent (and then sell) relatively small lots to small-to-medium size enterprises. (This was coupled with a special program to extend financial assistance to companies of those sizes.) Then in the late 1980s-early 1990s, greater prosperity returned and the CIC sites began to fill up (see photograph 18 for a typical factory site). The cost of land there rose further, relative to that of space in the rest of the metropolitan region, and more companies began to establish plants outside the Industrial City. By 1998 there were 535 factories in CIC, employing 50,000 directly (perhaps 200,000 indirectly outside the designated industrial park area) but a much larger number of (generally much smaller) new factories were established outside the Industrial City, in the southern part of Curitiba, as well as beyond the city limits. Nearly as many women were employed in CIC as men, whereas in the principal industrial park of Greater Belo Horizonte, dedicated primarily to heavy industry, more than 90 percent of the workers were male. CIC no longer offered the incentives of former days, and this was accentuated in the late 1980s when a state administration under the leadership of a party opposing the Lerner growth agenda decided to close BADEP, Paraná's development bank. (While businesses in Minas Gerais did not have to cope with any such closure of the state development entity there, which is reported to have lent $7 billion between 1972 and 1993[5], some of the reduction in credit available to activities in Paraná was offset by increased efforts to obtain funding for prospective investors from the Regional Bank of the Extreme South, a development institution that serves the three southernmost states of the country). Because Brazil was opening up its economy, local enterprises were subject to more competition than before. Yet a 1995 survey indicated, somewhat more than half of the firms in CIC lacked systems of quality control.[6] For many firms there was still a considerable lag in the learning experience.

Training and technical assistance measures were undertaken at the national level—and also by the State of Paraná and the City of Curitiba. To begin with, there was the national technical assistance service, SEBRAE, which was aimed at small to medium size enterprises. Other national programs existed as well. The most appreciated by industry were the evening and on-the-job training programs of SENAI, the national apprenticeship program. Also important were the handful of exceptionally equipped technical high schools affiliated with SENAI that turned out state-of-the-art technicians for the country's enterprises in metalworking, communications and several other specialties. These are located in a number of Brazilian cities although not in Curitiba. Students graduating from those programs are taken for visits to factories in the leading industrial centers of the country.

The State of Paraná contributed to the competitiveness of enterprises with TECPAR and with the affiliated program of Technological Incubators that was aimed at start-up, high technology enterprises (a program also supported by several federal entities and private groups including FIEP).[7] In turn, Curitiba's CIC promoted a number of programs—a partnership with SEBRAE to help develop suppliers and attract more to areas close to leading producers, a design training institute, a competitiveness center aimed at the MERCOSUR common market with Argentina, Uruguay, and Paraguay, a Seal of Quality Prize Program, a Business Information and Customs Center, and of special importance, a Software Park intended to help put enterprises on the technological frontier.

Small farms and sparsely populated areas were common even within the limits of the Municipality of Curitiba in 1966 when the *Guidelines* were approved. This is the major reason why so little is said in that document about the further, more distant reaches of the Metropolitan Curitiba Region. In 1973, Brazil designated a dozen metropolitan areas in the country and defined their geographical limits. That constituted an effort to get those in the principal cities of the country to coordinate their activities with the areas immediately surrounding them. At the time perhaps an eighth of the population of the Curitiba Metropolitan Region lived outside the city itself, most in several large towns, and the rest in much smaller communities or on farms. With the passage of the years several reasons emerged for integrating more of the activities of the region. First, until quite recently, the suburbs of Curitiba served largely as bedroom communities, with most of those with jobs having to travel every day to the Industrial City or other locations in Curitiba. The area outside the city limits had become increasingly part of the Curitiba community, but a part with a significantly lower income base because most of the major new factories and service activities still were located within the city limits of Curitiba. The bedroom communities beyond the city did not share in the tax revenues of the emerging Curitiba industrial base to the same extent as the city itself. One consequence of this was that the construction of urban infrastructure in those communities lagged badly and with the exception of a few areas, living conditions were much more rudimentary than in Curitiba.

Another consequence was that many of the problems of the outskirts inevitably reached into Curitiba. By the mid-1990s, more of the unemployed and the children of those who held meager positions made their way downtown, increasing the numbers engaged in begging or petty larceny. The arrival of a mounting number of buses from the suburbs that were not integrated into Curitiba's transport system and traveled into the center city undermined both the transportation solutions that the city had so carefully designed and the quality of the air.

By the 1990s there were two more consequences to take into account. First, with the large plots in CIC fast filling up and the price of its land no longer inexpensive, more of the new manufacturing plants were going to have to locate beyond the city limits if the metropolitan area's much vaunted economic expansion was to continue. It was recognized that installing industrial plants in twenty-five competitive and much less regulated communities outside Curitiba's city limits could well lead to harmful environmental effects, beginning with threats to the river basins that were located primarily outside the Curitiba city limits. Only a small part of the environment at risk was truly protected by legislation of the State of Paraná. (An early example of the problem presented itself in 1982. While Curitiba had been seeking non-polluting industries, Araucária, just west of the southern part of the city, landed a major petroleum refinery, thanks to the intervention of the state's political leaders. A decade later, as Curitiba neighborhoods bordering on Araucária began to gain substantially in population, air quality began to become a concern in those areas of Curitiba even though it remained quite high in most of the city.)

The first official recognition of the need for a metropolitan area approach, an accord among 13 mayors of the region, was signed in the mid-1960s but little came of it or of a document of the state government along similar lines a few years later. In 1974, within a year after its designation by the national government as a metropolitan area, the Curitiba Region Coordination Council (COMEC) was established. Initially, funding was dependent principally on federal sources, and as of the 1980s, on state and local sources, particularly after the changes specified in the Brazilian Constitution of 1988. Even so, political rivalries appear to explain the low level of funding prior to 1994. The first major structural effort, the Plan for Integrated Development of 1978, emphasized the preservation of natural resources, the creation of wealth (especially through industrialization), and the creation of regional sub-centers with urban services (only three of any consequence of which existed at the time). It was anticipated that the Curitiba transport system would encompass the entire metropolitan area, but that was thwarted both by political rivalries and the rapid growth in the population of the suburban communities that led to more decentralization of economic activity. It was not until 1996 that the integrated Curitiba system reached even the most prominent of the jurisdictions outside the city limits.

The first truly active participation of the City of Curitiba in COMEC appears to have taken place in 1983 with collaboration of IPPUC in regional health and education projects. Following that, the Municipal Development Plan of 1985 dealt with certain issues, but as mentioned, little came of that Plan. A 1991 report of the State of Paraná concerning the adverse effects of limestone quarry waste on the water supply led to the COMEC plan of 1992 and the establishment of a special office on the environment. An incinerator

for hospital waste was constructed and plans were drawn up for the relocation of families residing in river basin areas. The Metropolitan Curitiba Region (RMC) has never had funds for housing, though recently it began to
benefit from a state public housing program. As of late 1997, only 40 percent of the metropolitan area outside the city had adequately treated water
and only 25 percent, sewerage connections. Flooding remained as serious a
problem as it had been within the Curitiba city limits many years before. A
sense of the need for a regional approach also is revealed by the location of
new settlements; in Colombo, on the northern border of Curitiba, more than
90 percent of the population now live outside what had traditionally been
the political/administrative heart of the city as recently as the early 1990s.

By 1996, Curitiba Mayor Cassio Taniguchi met regularly with COMEC,
which, in turn, became closely linked with the planning offices of the state
government. COMEC was to make special efforts in the areas of environmental sanitation, preservation and recuperation of green spaces, physical
and urban infrastructure and the promotion of economic development. This
would include the establishment or improvement of industrial parks outside
Curitiba, such as the one in San José das Pinhas, to the southeast of the city.
All this, not a moment too soon. In March of that year, the Government of
Paraná convinced Renault to make a major investment in São José de Pinhas,
and this was followed by commitments from Chrysler, Audi-Volkswagen
and internationally prominent suppliers such as Detroit Diesel and Bertrand
Faure to locate in Curitiba's suburbs. By 1997 it appeared that the new
automobile related investments would amount to $2.5 billion, and between
1995 and 2001, all new industrial investments in Paraná totaled $20 billion,
most of which came from overseas and went to the Metropolitan Curitiba
Region. (A factor that contributed to these investments was the greater economic stability that Brazil was enjoying under the Plan Real, which went
into effect in 1994—though note: that greater economic stability was accompanied by an overvaluation of the local currency of 15-25 percent, a
factor adverse to foreign investment.) The exact value of the incentives
extended to individual foreign investors was never specified in public (a
major political controversy) and the reduced restrictions on land used for
the automobile assembly operations near river basins also were subject to
question. The RMC already had accounted for half of Paraná's manufacturing value added in the late 1980s and that may have risen to 60 percent
by the end of the 1990s. While more jobs in the Curitiba area now require
high school education or higher, new migrants to the RMC numbered 100,000
a year in the last half of the 1990s according to unofficial estimates, and

most of the newly arriving labor force do not possess the level of educational background being sought by the new industrial installations.

Assistance in expanding the infrastructure and organizational needs of the RMC outside the city limits of Curitiba became available from an on-going statewide project of municipal development. See especially Lowry 2002. The first phase was initiated by Governor Ney Braga in 1981-82 and was influenced in part by the Curitiba experience, with Lubomir Ficinski, one of key members of the Lerner Group in charge. The dimensions of the project were increased during the period 1984-95 with the support of the World Bank, the activities then being financed by loans instead of grants, as at first. The Inter-American Development Bank provided the principal source of financing from 1996 through 2000 with Ficinski returning to head up this stage. Paraná Urbano, as this third stage was known, supported Governor Lerner's "Integration Ring" of highways in the middle of the state, and also contributed to the paving of streets and other basic infrastructure in municipalities other than Curitiba throughout the state. In contrast to the Curitiba approach, this program of regional development left a good deal up to the criteria of the individual communities. While Lowry supports the concept of the municipal development undertaken and a number of the specific results, he indicates that more can be said about the use of cost-benefit criteria ex ante than about the overall results ex post. Neither a municipality's economic nor administrative performance played a significant role in the allocation of funds, however.

By the end of the 1990s, reference to Curitiba had come to mean the Metropolitan Curitiba Region. The city and the state were marshalling new efforts for the region; Curitiba had become a larger and more complex community. By the same token, the challenges seemed more difficult and official publicity no longer trumpeted the claims made in the early 1990s about the quality of life to quite the same extent.

Transportation

As much as Curitiba prides itself on its dual purpose parks and unique urban landscape, few abroad might be taking special note of the city had it not been for its singularly successful achievements in public transportation.

Relatively little change took place in public transport between 1982 and 1988. One modification, though, which helped assure that it would be profitable for the private companies to operate as the city sought, serving remote as well as populous precincts, was the decision in 1986 to compensate private operators on the basis of mileage rather than the number of passengers transported. A second was IPPUC's development of the "tubular" bus station in 1984—though that was not implemented until the Lerner Group returned to office.

When Lerner became mayor again in 1989, his group focused first on the public transit system.[8] The private bus companies had been required to replace the 60 to 80 passenger buses of the 1960s with others able to carry 110 passengers, and, on the main traffic arteries, 170 passengers. Still, this did not seem to resolve problems well enough. It was recognized that commuter traffic, though increasing, was leveling off and was not sufficient to justify an underground subway system. Considerable interest evolved in a light rail system that would allow transport of up to 660 passengers per vehicle but cost only a fifth of a subway system. Nonetheless, concerns about rerouting bus traffic during a two year construction period, building an underground station in the center of the city (necessary because of grade considerations) and difficulties in obtaining financing because of probable costs, all led to an abandonment of the light rail project.

At that point, the city turned to an upgraded version of bus transportation that captured some of the features of light rail. URBS redesigned both the buses and bus stops and arranged for the payment of bus fares prior to boarding, at the entrance of the tubular bus stations that IPPUC had proposed. URBS President Carlos Ceneviva then convinced Volvo's Curitiba plant to manufacture two and three section (articulated and biarticulated) vehicles, the later designed to carry up to 270 passengers (able to accommodate 300 if necessary). Each of the two (or three) bus sections was constructed with five doors, each door with two movable side plates twice as large as a traditional door. The driver could lower the plates and the entire door to form a bridge, enabling even large numbers of passengers to board or leave the bus in a fraction of the time required for the descending from ordinary buses. The Volvo chassis were combined with bodies built by the Rio Grande do Sul factory, Marco Polo. The result was a system that could transport up to 25,800 passengers per hour on the principal lines if necessary, more than the city has required, even at peak hours. Modernistic tempered glass and steel tubes replaced the earlier fiberglass and trellis shelters, providing even better protection against inclement weather. The tubes were manufactured locally and could be mounted in a few hours. Passengers entered the tubes by paying their fare and passing through a turnstile, waiting there for the bus. This eliminated delay in bus departure because of the need to collect fares, shortening the total time required for given trips (which reduced average fuel consumption and pollution emissions) and substantially reducing the number of buses required (and thus, the capital requirements of the transportation system). In addition, it eliminated the custom of having a second person in each bus to collect fares (as continued to be the custom in the conventional buses still in use in the city).

Whereas it was estimated that the light rail project would have cost $280 million for the 18 kilometer North-South line, the new Curitiba system, fully implemented, involved an outlay of only $48 million, less than a fifth as much. A loan for the project from the Inter-American Development Bank enabled the city to extend platform-level boarding into new areas of Curitiba (which entailed remodeling half a dozen existing terminals and constructing four new ones). In addition, the loan financed a doubling of the percentage of bus routes whose entire extension is properly paved, drained and illuminated, as well as other improvements, including the construction of six user-support facilities built around existing terminal structures. The user support facilities include bank branch offices, pharmacies, municipal services (even training and social services), a library, indoor sports areas, beverage outlets and newsstands.

As of the year 2000, Curitiba had 165 of the new two or three section bus lines in its Integrated Transport System and 87 stand-alone commuter lines. In addition, there were 34 special education lines (2 for handicapped children), 2 lines for handicapped adults, 1 inter-hospital line, 1 that made a circular run in the downtown area, and another dedicated to tourism. Private companies are responsible for purchasing the vehicles and undertaking the maintenance that the city deems necessary while the city provides the basic infrastructure—approximately 45 miles of exclusive bus lanes, 21 terminals and 221 tubular stations. Daily passenger trips number 1.9 million—600,000 of which involve full fares, and the rest, transfers and subsidized fares such as for the elderly and handicapped. Whereas 90 percent of those traveling from one part of the city to another cross-town passed through downtown at the inauguration of the interdistrict buses, only 52 per cent do at present. Buses are replaced at least every ten years. A major extension of the system to include the nearby jurisdictions of Metropolitan Curitiba is currently underway.

The existing bus system is color coded, with no visible indication of the ten private companies involved. The Red Lines are modernistic two and three section buses that operate in the exclusive lanes set in the middle of relatively wide major North-South, East West, Boqueirão and South Circular traffic arteries. Tubular glass and steel stations are located approximately

400 meters apart and terminals with connections to other lines, at approximately five-kilometer intervals. The new Red Line three section vehicles with their tubular station arrangement have the lowest unit costs and were featured at the 1995 UN Conference on the Environment in Ankara, Turkey. A variation of the Curitiba arrangement has been adopted, or is being considered by Quito, Ecuador, Bogotá, Colombia and São Paulo, and eighteen cities in the United States.

The Silver Line features express buses that make fewer stops (every three kilometers) but do not travel in exclusive (dedicated) lanes. Orange Lines are feeder buses that service lower density areas, stop every two to three blocks, and connect with other bus lines in terminals. Green Line buses traverse circular routes between neighborhoods and connect in terminals with Red, Silver and Orange buses. Free transfer between buses of the various lines is available at any of the terminals and at other specified transfer points. Some manufacturing plants in CIC without a municipal bus stop adjacent to their facility, operate private buses, either to a nearby terminal or to other areas of the city. Travel by bus in Curitiba is more pleasant and relatively more utilized by the middle class than in other Latin American cities, most notably on the Red Lines. Despite late 1990s data indicating that Curitiba passed Brasilia as the city registering the highest rate of automobile ownership in the major cities of the country, an estimated that 70-75 percent of those going to work travel by bus.

---

[1]   Jaime Lerner comments:

In 1988, I won my first election as mayor. As a politician, I was a freshman. I would have a long way ahead before even wishing to think of running for president. My only concern, as Brazil was in severe economic difficulties, was to guarantee that Curitiba would be able to continue its development, maintaining the quality of life for its population, which was increasing rapidly.

We invested a lot in housing and created several programs such as the lots of land for low-income people. "Bairro Novo" [The New Neighborhood], launched in 1991, provided lots with urban infrastructure to 10,000 families and houses to 20,000 more. Today it is practically a city.

In those years, needy people and their children were a concern since many mothers started to work to help the family, which was not yet traditional in Brazil. Within the scope of programs focusing on children, we created 30 integral education centers where students might go full time or part time, after school hours. The objective was to keep children busy with recreation, sports and research activities, in addition to providing meals, so that they would not loiter in the streets.

The creation of the Day Care Center Voucher widened the social programs focused on children. Small and large companies started buying places in public day care centers, assisting their workers and funding the creation of new units, in addition to new places for children from poor communities. All day care centers were equipped with pre-school facilities.

Another highlight was the creation of 24-Hour Health Care Center Units, with emergency medical and dental care and facilities for minor surgery and short-term stays.

Of course, ecology was also a major concern, so we designed programs geared to the environment and better quality of life. The main icons of the third term are the "Speedy" buses, the "Garbage that is not Garbage" program and the Open University for the Environment-UNILIVRE. Lerner 2003.

[2] See, for example, Menezes 1996, 148 and Appendix B of this book.

[3] Two aspects of the land use legislation should be noted: first, buildings beyond the downtown area were required to be set back five meters from the main street. Second, construction was to be allowed on only 50 percent of the area of residential plots and the open spaces were not to be covered in a manner that would prevent them from absorbing water runoffs (this to reduce the threat of flooding).

[4] On legitimization processes, see Kleindorfer, Kunreuther and Schoemaker 1993.

[5] Eakin 2001, 154 and 232.

[6] A more extensive survey of productivity, in this case of enterprises throughout the State of Paraná was completed in 1998 by the Japanese funded Brazilian Institute of Quality and Productivity.

[7] See also the study on the competitiveness of industry in Paraná, IPARDES 1994.

[8] What follows draws heavily on Wright 1996b, Unknown Compiler 1999, Ceneviva [1999?], del Santoro 2000, written comments of Wright to an earlier draft in March 2001, and U.S. Department of Transportation 2001.

7

The Private Sector Response

For most of the past century Curitiba was a city in which government, university and commercial activity were the mainstays, with traditional agroindustry also of consequence. The latter revolved around the local green tea (yerba mate), foodstuffs generally, coffee as of the 1940s, and lumber and furniture. Brazil's major industrial outposts lie northeast of the city, in São Paulo, Rio de Janeiro and Belo Horizonte, and to the south, in Porto Alegre, with a group of nationally competitive smaller entrepreneurs situated immediately south of the state's borders, in less populous Joinville and Blumenau.

Eastern Paraná's forests were fast disappearing but at mid-century the state remained eminently agricultural. There were the well-known market crops and a sizable subsistence agriculture sector that was becoming more market-oriented. And there was the "new agricultural frontier" in the northern, western, and southwestern parts of the state. Those areas had attracted the largest rural-oriented migration in all Brazil between 1940 and 1960, a phenomenon chronicled by the American agricultural economist, William Nicholls. On those few occasions when politicians from Paraná were recognized and rewarded nationally, it tended to be with the designation as Minister of Agriculture.

As for modern industry, the state scarcely registered on Brazil's horizon and the efforts in the 1960s to promote industries geared primarily to the local market certainly did not alter that. Prototypical perhaps, was the tale of two nineteenth century German metalworking immigrants. One headed for Porto Alegre, where he established what became an important steel mill, while the other journeyed to Curitiba, where he set up a metalworking shop that prospered initially but eventually became the site of the shopping center referred to earlier. Even in the mid-to-late 1990s, old-timers in the Federation of Industries of the State of Paraná (FIEP), spoke with a certain air of times past, when most factories were small and based on the output of the fields, when production processes were simple, major concerns with production efficiency the exception, and technological change seldom mentioned. The transformation from that laid back environment to the Curitiba of the 1990s in less than a generation was beyond anyone's imagination, and while capital from beyond the region accounted for much of what has transpired, a number of domestic enterprises also were actively involved.

Several factors have contributed to the extraordinary response of private enterprise during the period between 1970 and the close of the 20th Century, even among locals, who had been reticent to undertake ambitious new projects in the past. The earlier attitudes began to change after 1970. This may have reflected the wrenching transformation the state underwent in the 1960s and 1970s. More important, though, was the suddenly rapidly growing and more modern local economy, driven increasingly by the investors from beyond Curitiba's borders. However, before considering the reasons set forth by private enterprises for investing in Curitiba, recall first, the major effort that local government made to alter development patterns.

The contribution of those government initiatives went beyond the addition of socioeconomic infrastructure that had been lacking and the provision of incentives that competed with those being offered by the Minas Gerais, Rio Grande do Sul, and other states. Of perhaps greater consequence, the energetic and ever-more-effective "Marketing of Curitiba" led an increasing number of enterprises from abroad, from Greater São Paulo and from elsewhere in Brazil to first consider Curitiba as a site for modern industry—to even bother to estimate the relative advantages of locating there. This seems to have been overlooked by many of those who characterize the city's remarkable industrial transformation as no more than what should have been anticipated from rational economic decision making, taking location and all of the financial pluses and minuses into account.

The latter, economically rational line of reasoning assumes that those who decided to invest in Curitiba had been aware of essentially all of the relevant information, that they had perceived that information accurately, and that they were able to utilize it in calculating what was in their best interest. Studies that document how common it is for those who intend to perform well and who have incentives to do so, to experience difficulty in realizing that objective, and how important the *framing* of information is to the effectiveness with which that information is employed are summarized in Schwartz 1998 and Schwartz 2003. (Those references also indicate the sources that document the importance of framing to the type of decision rules that are triggered in lieu of the careful calculation of optimization techniques.)

Marketing certainly can make a difference, and there is good reason to believe that in the case of Curitiba, it did. It alerted many foreign enterprises to Curitiba's advantages (which were indeed increasing for a good many years). Beyond that, the colorful, exuberant marketing also may have led some investors to regard the city more favorably vis-à-vis other locales than strictly rational considerations would have called for.

This chapter is based in part on extensive written materials and numerous casual conversations over the course of several months each in 1995, 1997 and 1998, but primarily on in-depth interviews with producers.[1] What follows draws on only one component of those often fascinating exchanges— that dealing with their decisions to expand in or to relocate to the Curitiba area.

The Attitude Toward Investment and Entrepreneurship as of the 1960s

Local producers and other businessmen seemed to have been inclined to keep their profits at home—more so than in most other regions of Brazil. Some of the more successful businesses in the State of Paraná did relocate their headquarters from smaller communities in the state to Curitiba, but unlike the case of lawyers, architects and other professionals, not many sought the bigger ponds of São Paulo or Rio. Also, few chose to follow in the footsteps of the successful small-to-medium size enterprises from Santa Catarina and produce for truly national markets. Most accounts suggest that producers from Paraná were not especially concerned with modern management techniques and were not very entrepreneurially oriented.[2] In those days, few Brazilian initiatives could be traced to Curitiba, and only a handful of enterprises responded with much imagination to the added economic infrastructure provided by the state government or the greatly expanded development financing of the state as well as national governments in the mid-to-late 1960s. Moreover, even in the Brazilian "Miracle Growth" period of 1968-73, perspectives in Paraná must have been in doubt, given the collapsing coffee production and the extraordinary internal migration that was taking place. Risk taking and a more entrepreneurial disposition began to play a more important role among local producers only after enterprises from outside the region began to invest in Curitiba. At that point, there does appears to have been a change in mentality, a change in the disposition to attempt more than before and to alter the approach to decision making, accompanied by a tendency to think in terms of national and international markets.

Government Intervention

The State Government provided the initial impetus for the change, as already noted. In the 1960s, the first major highway between Curitiba and São Paulo was constructed along with other important roads, and notable additions were made to the electric power grid—an essential contribution of government, given the restrictions on the private profitability of such undertakings. In the 1970s, CIC, the largest, greenest and probably most costly industrial park in Latin America was constructed, and Curitiba began to compete with other cities in terms of the incentives offered for new investment. A majority of Latin American industrial parks in industrial backwaters had been stark failures, however (even the first major one in Greater Belo Horizonte did not find enterprises to utilize all of the available space for a quarter of a century) and, as for most of the other incentives, they were hardly unique to Curitiba; the tax postponements and exemptions did not differ from those offered elsewhere according to businessmen.

The increasing pollution and the generally growing diseconomies of Metropolitan São Paulo helps explain why much new investment, Brazilian as well as foreign, would head elsewhere, but why to Curitiba, why not to another closer community in the State of São Paulo, or in neighboring Minas Gerais? Why not to the cities of Santa Catarina, which though somewhat more distant, boasted a solid industrial base and superior support services? Indeed, if to Paraná, why not to Londrina, which, during the State's coffee boom of the 40s, 50s and 60s, had become closely linked to São Paulo, and which suddenly had an abundance of people seeking employment? All of these communities did experience new industrial investment, but none of the relative magnitude of Curitiba. Of the large and medium size metropolitan centers of Brazil, it is in Curitiba that the most rapid growth of industry took place during the last three decades of the twentieth century.

Why did private businessmen respond so demonstrably?

With respect to the 1970s, the explanations offered here are based on the surveys referred to in Chapter 1, along with the recall of several entrepreneurs interviewed during the period 1995-98. For the relatively lean years of the 1980s, what follows is based mainly on the interviews. For the 1990s, the account draws from the interviews and also from public accounts, principally those appearing in several Curitiba newspapers and in the national financial journal, *A Gazeta do Comércio*. Note will be taken of the response of some successful local enterprises but since decision making in those enterprises was much influenced by the successes of enterprises newly arrived from beyond the region, particular attention will be given to the latter, examining the reasons that they offered for locating in Curitiba. Synthesizing, the reasons for locating and/or reinvesting in Curitiba seem to be the following:

- Relatively good access to the country's major market, the São Paulo-Rio-Belo Horizonte triangle or, in a few cases, good access to important regional markets.
- Investment incentives of approximately the same level offered by other metropolitan areas.
- Educational resources that were fairly good and improving.
- Lower pay scales for all levels of labor skill (including engineers and managers) than in the country's major industrial centers.
- Municipal promoters apparently somewhat more adept than those from most other cities in linking foreign investors to national incentive schemes and in attending to special interests of individual foreign investors.
- The capacity, continuity, integrity and vision of leading public officials.
- Improving, if still limited industrial support systems (suppliers, special services).
- Quality of Life: Curitiba made extensive claims about the city's Quality of Life in the late 1980s and in the 1990s, and it is at about that time that it became a more significant factor in decisions to invest in the city. A few companies that relocated to Curitiba tended to downplay this factor in their decision, but two factors lend credence to the case for Quality of Life considerations. First, Curitiba's lower pay scales, while undoubtedly due in part to its more agricultural and public sector background (still important in the 1970s), and to its lack of a strong labor union tradition, also was attributable in part to the level of public amenities and the social welfare safety net, particularly by the late 1980s. This was mentioned by many enterprises, particularly with respect to the public amenities and the lower cost of achieving what was regarded as a good standard of living. Second, all enterprises were going to have to pay full local taxes three to five years after the initiation of their investment or expansion yet not a single company interviewed raised objections about the high level of public expenditures for parks,

civic improvements and social welfare programs in the city. This certainly amounts to implicit acceptance of the Quality of Life argument. The level of public expenditure for parks, civic improvements and social welfare programs, taken together, probably constituted a higher percentage of the total municipal budget than in any major city in Brazil. Certainly this was true of what might be characterized as the public parks and monuments component, as those in the political opposition often complained.

• Marketing: Marketing programs first brought most of these factors to the attention of companies from abroad and from other areas of Brazil. Many firms did not include Curitiba in the comparisons they made of investment sites until after the early 1970s. By the 1990s Curitiba was more commonly taken into account in attempting to determine the most appropriate location for a new or expanded plant, although the successful eleventh hour entry of Curitiba into the discussions surrounding the Renault automobile assembly plant in 1995-96 reveals that this was still not always the case. The weighting of what was stressed may have changed by the 1990s, but marketing remained important in making sure that those not familiar with the Metropolitan Curitiba region took it into consideration before making their investment decisions.

The Arrival of Large Foreign Enterprises in Curitiba

The decision to attempt to attract large foreign firms and the success in achieving that goal distinguished Curitiba's efforts from those of cities in neighboring Santa Catarina, and was the key to what transpired in the generation that followed. Minas Gerais also attracted large foreign firms, primarily to exploit the state's mineral resources and help initiate a steel industry, but in the 1970s, two-thirds of all industrial investment in Minas came from the state government and only a fifth from foreign capital. In Paraná, the state did not provide any of the investment in industry, the overwhelming share coming from the foreign firms. The nine enterprises interviewed from outside the region all were in branches of industry that differed from the dominant endeavors of Paraná past. Eight were foreign owned and one, a Brazilian facility that relocated from São Paulo. One firm produced electrical equipment, one telecommunications materials, and another equipment for pulping and for underwater petroleum exploration. Three metalworking establishments were oriented primarily towards parts for transportation equipment, one company manufactured trucks and buses and two were automobile assembly plants that first began construction of their facilities in 1997.

The reasons cited by the enterprises for relocating to Curitiba or for undertaking additional investments there varied from one decade to the next. The CIC incentive of inexpensive land with excellent infrastructure was cited by all four of the interviewed firms that moved to Curitiba in the 1970s. Two emphasized the importance of this incentive, one was more moderate in its enthusiasm, and the fourth contended that, while a positive factor, the incentive was not critical.[3] One of the firms, while acknowledging the value of the incentives, maintained that several states extended roughly comparable incentives. Another commented that the value of state and local incentives was smaller than that obtained from the federal government for relocating to any site beyond Greater São Paulo. The same was true of the tax incentives, to which two of the four firms also assigned importance. The marketing and promotional capability of the Municipality of Curitiba was mentioned by two of the four firms and might have been mentioned by all four had the interviews been held twenty years earlier with more of those directly involved, judging by the remarks of one of the more successful Curitiba-based enterprises whose key personnel had remained the same throughout the entire period. The quality and cost of human resources was stressed by one firm and mentioned relatively favorably by two others, in one case, because initially there was a lack of local competition for the most skilled professionals and laborers, and in two cases, because labor unions were characterized as less aggressive than in São Paulo. Finally, three of the four firms commented on the importance of local infrastructure.

The two interviewed firms that came to Curitiba in the 1980s cited Curitiba's marketing and promotional capability as the leading reason for their move. In one case, this was combined with the goal of becoming a supplier of one of the major corporations already there, an objective that the Curitiba authorities were energetically encouraging. Both firms also mentioned one additional, less important factor (a different one in each case).

As for the 1990s, 7 of the 9 firms mentioned the importance of the city's Quality of Life in explaining why they came to or continued to expand in Curitiba. Two speculated that this factor might have peaked, but another said that in its view, Curitiba paid more attention to future needs than the other two cities it had most carefully considered. No other explanation for relocating to Curitba was voiced by more than two or three firms, but among the reasons obtaining at least that level of support were the following: the improving training facilities, the improving capability of local suppliers (which the new arrivals themselves helped to foster), inexpensive land (by then, primarily unsubsidized and outside the city limits), and the quality/cost combination of human resources, which was judged by most to be attributable to the local work ethic but perhaps even more, to less combative labor unions. Of those that came to Curitba in the 1990s, only one firm expressly mentioned the importance of Curitiba's marketing efforts— but that was *in addition* to Renault, for which energetic, successful marketing indeed appears to have been the critical explanation for the decision to establish a facility in Curitiba.

So much of what took place during the last part of the twentieth century was influenced by the arrival of large foreign corporations in Curitiba in the 1970s and their on-going expansion that it is useful to give somewhat further attention to the reasoning of several of those enterprises. Consider the case of the Siemens Group, two companies of which decided to locate in Curitiba, along with Volvo and Kvaerner Pulping.

Siemens and Equitel: Electronic Equipment, Telecommunications (German). Already active in Brazil, the Siemens Group first established a branch office in Curitiba in the 1930s and then again in 1956. In 1973, one of the enterprises of the Group established a plant in Curitiba to produce a wide range of engineering products and a second made a commitment to locate in the industrial city then under construction. Business and cultural ties played a part in the decision to come to Curitiba (the city had a fairly large and prominent population of German ancestry), but the promotional role of Mayor Jaime Lerner and his group was deemed more important. Related to that, company officials cited the importance of the city's restructured public transport and particularly its educational infrastructure—its public school system and its engineering faculties, both of which were regarded as better than in another municipality that was being considered at the time. Inexpensive land was important in the decision to locate the Equitel factory in CIC, though less so in the case of the Siemens facility nearer downtown. Equitel also was greatly influenced by its desire to be near TELEPAR, the State telephone company from whom it had begun to obtain contracts for telecommunications equipment. Some mention was made of local fiscal incentives, but more of the initially favorable infrastructure and the efforts in the mid-1990s to further upgrade infrastructure. Those factors, what was regarded as an energetic and imaginative workforce, and the favorable Quality of Life contributed to the decision of Siemens in the 1990s to select Curitiba as one of the sites for its worldwide R and D operations.

Volvo: Truck Assembly (Swedish). Volvo set up a facility in Curitiba in 1977, and the first vehicle rolled off its assembly line in 1979. Incentives of the federal government to decentralize away from the São Paulo area led the company to consider a number of sites, with the final determination between Curitiba and Campinas, the well known university center in the interior of the State of São Paulo. Curitiba's distance from the principal markets was judged to be adequate, even though greater than that of Campinas. The city's overall infrastructure was judged to be better, with special reference to Curitiba's access to maritime and airport facilities. Labor unions were deemed less aggressive in Curitiba. Fiscal benefits and the subsidy in the price of land apparently were similar. Finally, a major consideration was the more accommodating and less bureaucratic manner of city and state officials. The Quality of Life was considered as a positive, but minor factor at the time of the initial decision. Volvo was motivated to continue investing in Paraná in the 1990s for several reasons. The situation with respect to suppliers had improved greatly, the worker pool was more qualified than at the outset and absenteeism low, and the local market for its trucks had become relatively more important. By the beginning of the 1990s, the Quality of Life argument figured more importantly, and the opinion was voiced that Curitiba paid more attention to future civic needs than other cities.

Kvaerner Pulping: Equipment for Making Pulp and Offshore Petroleum Exploration Equipment (Norwegian, Swedish, Finnish and British). Kvaerner established a sales office in São Paulo in 1974, and, motivated by Brazilian restrictions on imports, built a manufacturing plant in Curitiba in 1977. The company also has factories in Sweden, Canada and the United States. The leadership of the Brazilian plant claimed that a number of its products were competitive with Kvaerner facilities overseas in 1997-98 (despite a currency overvaluation of 25-30%) and provided some supporting evidence. The decision to locate outside São Paulo was influenced by the Federal Government incentives regarding decentralization. Several locations were considered and initially, land was even purchased for a site between São Paulo and Rio. The decision to turn instead to Curitiba was based principally on three factors. First, manpower: the availability and quality of manpower (half of whom would be engineers and technical school graduates) and the ease with which the less skilled workforce could be trained, coupled with the absence of what were characterized as "aggressive" labor unions. Second, the most important individual customer of the firm in Brazil was located in Paraná. A third influence was the relatively greater European culture in Curitiba than in other sites considered. Subsidized land and tax incentives were not judged to be greater than elsewhere. Once established, there was of course a strong financial force for continuing in Curitiba. This was reinforced by the increasing ease of convincing technical and management specialists to move to Curitiba (in part a reflection of the Quality of Life argument), and by the increase in the local market for the firm's products as a percentage of overall sales in Brazil. Those factors more than offset concerns that the firm had in the mid-to-late 1980s and in the beginning of the 1990s about the deterioration of certain CIC infrastructure (notably roads).

The Response of Local Producers Well Established Before 1970

Raw material supplies together with market considerations explained the location of five of the seven pre-1970 local private producers interviewed— two in woodworking, one in dairying (a cooperative), one in chemicals and one in plastic products. In addition, there was a firm whose origins were somewhat related to agroindustry, a manufacturer of refrigerators, which had evolved into one of the few local enterprises of national scope. The seventh firm was engaged in construction and in the commercial management of some of the facilities it had built. Also interviewed: several middle level managers of the state electric power company, established in 1963.

None of the seven private companies have considered a move away from Curitiba. Available natural resources, the attraction of a familiar and rapidly expanding local market, and ownership by locally-oriented, relatively risk averse families all go a long way to explaining this. One of the companies also cited the favorable socioeconomic infrastructure, another, the improving training facilities in the city, and two firms, the favorable Quality of Life. Five of the firms still operated in their pre-1970 plants outside the industrial park (outside the city limits, in one case), but one enterprise had taken advantage of the favorable price of land in CIC and a second was at long last planning to relocate to an alternative, larger and lower cost location in the Curitiba area. Tax incentives were cited by only one enterprise, which claimed, nonetheless, that federal tax benefits were much greater. That firm also was one of two to mention the enticement of

favorable terms of credit, the latter apparently in conjunction with an anticipated merger with a foreign enterprise. On the other hand, one of this pre-
1970 group of firms argued against the wisdom of borrowing and maintained that it had never done so, even when the rates were subsidized.

Here, too, it is useful to look somewhat more at the situation of several
individual firms.

Berneck: Woodworking, primarily plywood and veneer. Woodworking
and furniture accounted for approximately 25% of Curitiba's industrial value
added as late as the early 1970s but by the mid-1990s, the figure was only
about 8%. Most of this decline was attributable to the large volume of new
investments in other branches of industry. However, the increasing defores-
tation of Eastern Paraná also played a role, as did the fact that many of the
leaders in the woodworking industry did not possess training in modern
woodworking technology or modern business techniques. Most of those firms
closed their doors and ceased to exist. Among the exceptions was Berneck.

Begun as a commercial operation in a small community in Paraná in
1936, Berneck opened a sawmill in 1946 and relocated to Curitiba in 1961
because of the city's greater access to lumber supplies and electric power.
National incentives to export in the 1970s led to further expansion and a
new site was purchased in CIC. At one point the firm operated 10 small
sawmills, but by the late 1990s, greater attention to technology and scale
operations had reduced the number to seven. Plans were underway to enter
into a joint venture with a large foreign concern that was to double capacity
even while reducing the number of plants to four. Berneck took advantage
of the incentives offered by local authorities. The firm's recognition of the
importance of new technology was accentuated by the presence among
their CIC neighbors of the increasingly higher technology firms that had
come to Curitiba. Moreover, Berneck's location in the by-then-famous
Curitiba Industrial City may have been a factor in attracting the attention of
the foreign corporation with which it planned to merge.

Brasholanda: Plastic Containers. Brasholanda also began operations in a
smaller community in Paraná, and moved to Curitiba in the 1960s because
of the city's more strategic location between its raw material supply, to the
south, and its principal market, to the northeast in Greater São Paulo.
Brasholanda's decision to continue its expansion in Curitiba was explained
by several factors. While the company benefited from a subsidized plant
site, tax benefits and subsidized development banks credits, it insisted that

all of these were of the same order as it would have been able to obtain elsewhere. More importance was attributed to the cost of labor (estimated by the firm to be 40% lower than in the São Paulo area in the 1970s), the training facilities in the city (which it required for its increasingly technical operations), and what it characterized as the quality and less bureaucratic character of local government. As for the Quality of Life of the city itself, the executive interviewed said that it was a minor factor in explaining the firm's decision to continue in Curitiba. Moreover, he went on to observe that there were two Curitibas and implied that the Quality of Life in some of the neighborhoods of Curitiba was little better than in other Brazilian cities. Indeed, he indicated, as did those in several other companies, that he expected Curitiba's Quality of Life to decline in the period ahead.

Refripar: Refrigerators and Other Domestic Appliances. Founded in Curitiba more than fifty years ago, Refripar had become one of the leading manufacturers of domestic appliances in Brazil by the time it was sold to Electrolux, a foreign multinational, in December 1995. Although Refripar had opened two other factories in Brazil, it continued to base its operations in Curitiba, due in part to family ties but also because of the city's favorable infrastructure (highways, communications, access to port) and its satisfaction with the workforce there. Refripar benefited from subsidized credits from the local development bank but did not move to a new site in CIC. Electrolux, on the other hand, was planning to expand to a second location in the city, this one in the Industrial City (though sites were no longer subsidized by that time). The company concluded that the various incentives were as good as elsewhere in Brazil and the "social charges" to the wage bill somewhat lower than in alternative municipal locations that were serious site alternatives. The Electrolux representative commented on the favorable human resources in the plant (which had helped enable the facility to become ISO 9000 qualified) and in Curitiba generally, and the by then, satisfactory number of reliable suppliers.

The Addition of New Local Firms After 1970

Seven of the firms interviewed were established in their current form after 1970, though in one case, operation as a commercial entity had begun two years before, and in another, a modest manufacturing endeavor had been initiated in 1968. Of the five principal enterprises, only one was even remotely tied to agroindustry—a producer of biscuits and chocolates that had moved its operations (initially only commercial) to Curitiba from a small town in the state (and to Curitiba rather than to geographically more convenient Maringá because of the presence of the state capital and the Federal University of Paraná in Curitiba).[4] One of the other firms, a machine shop, served primarily as a supplier to the enterprises that had arrived recently from São Paulo or abroad but also produced for a few similar entities beyond the immediate vicinity. The other three relatively large companies manufactured products aimed especially at the growing and increasingly higher income local market, though they also looked to national and international markets. The production of this group included antennas, equipment for cellulose and paper products, and a wide range of products related to the fields of energy and telecommunications. This company producing the latter products emerged as one of the Brazilian leaders in its field. Indeed, while foreign firms were buying up many other local enterprises, this firm acquired a number of the plants of prominent foreign corporations.

Four and possibly all five of the relatively large firms viewed their location and continuation in Curitiba as related to the arrival of many large firms from outside the area and the major economic expansion that this was producing.[5] One of the five larger enterprises, when confronted with serious competitive threats from national and foreign producers in the early 1990s, reoriented its product mix and turned in a major way to subcontracting—all from local firms. Others also increased their reliance on outsourcing, similarly, almost entirely with local firms. Industries did not seek to cut costs by moving or seeking suppliers in lower income areas of the country (or abroad) as did many enterprises in other countries and even some from São Paulo.[6] Finally, two recently created smaller companies were interviewed, one in wood products and the other in construction materials. These, too, were motivated by the arrival of firms from São Paulo and the booming local economy, which the latter were helping to expand.

Four factors were most cited by this group of firms for initiating and then continuing major undertakings in Curitiba, To begin with, almost all of the enterprise leaders were from Curitiba and perceived information about the local potential more accurately than that relating to other communities. Second, three of the four large firms that started up in the 1970s cited rapidly growing local or regional demand as their most (or their second most) important reason for initiating their activities in Curitiba. Both firms that started up in the 1980s echoed that line of reasoning for that decade and also for the 1990s. The third most important reason cited, at least for the 1970s, was the availability of incentives. Inexpensive land and tax and credit incentives were mentioned by two of the four major firms that began operations in the 1970s, with special note, in the case of one enterprise, of the substantial economic infrastructure that accompanied land in the CIC. One of the two 1980s start-ups cited the mix of incentives in that decade. (For the 1990s, only one of the seven firms gave special mention to the importance of land incentives and only one to a mix of other incentives.)

The fourth most important reason mentioned for initiating or continuing activities in Curitiba, but the most important by the 1990s, was the increased availability of dependable suppliers and training facilities. Just behind that in importance for the decade, were rapidly expanding local demand and the quality and cost of human resources. The latter was attributed to various factors, but especially to "less aggressive" labor unions. The character of local government—its stability, consistency and integrity, was mentioned, principally by the firms that initiated activities in the 1970s. Two enterprises cited the importance of the Curitiba's Quality of Life as a reason for their expansion in the 1990s. The quality and cost of raw materials was cited as important by only one firm in each of the decades.

Again, a brief account of several individual firms:

Hubner: Machine shop with specialization in the transportation and agricultural machinery industries. Hubner was founded in 1980 as a small machine shop. The company set up a facility in CIC in 1983 with the assistance of a loan from BADEP, the state development bank. Both the loan and the land purchase reflected subsidies. Nonetheless, the key consideration is that the enterprise was established in order to service the expanding number of major new industrial plants arriving in the metropolitan area, and to take advantage of the technical assistance that they might provide. The latter proved to be considerable, given Hubner's strong interest in upgrading the standards of its output and the prevailing lack of suitable suppliers in the 1980s. Hubner is now a large, modern machine shop that operates three shifts a day. It has developed a substantial market in other areas of Brazil and exported approximately 7% of its output in 1995-97 despite the overvalued exchange rate.

SUND Emba BHS: Machinery for the paper and cellulose industries. Increased restrictions on importing machinery for the paper and cellulose industries in 1976 led to the establishment that year of SUND Emba by a group of Curitiba businessmen, in conjunction with a Swedish and then a

German manufacturer. When the latter two enterprises decided to export to Brazil, even while continuing to receive technology royalties from SUND Emba, the Brazilian firm opted to create an independent line of products aimed at small and medium size firms and to emphasize equipment servicing. Accompanying this, SUND Emba shifted from manufacturing 90% of its components in-house to a 90% dependence on subcontracting, almost entirely from micro enterprises of former employees whom it laid off. The company purchased a site in CIC but neither its start-up nor its revised activity in Curitiba appears to have been greatly affected by special incentives. Even so, the firm's ability to find markets for its products and new servicing activity was facilitated by the growing number of firms in Curitiba, some of who had been attracted to the city by incentives or who had been attracted to serve as suppliers to those who had responded to them.

INEPAR: Energy and Telecommunications Products. INEPAR, one of the leading Brazilian enterprises in its field in the 1990s, was established in 1968, but its major activity dates to the early-to-mid 1970s, after its relocation to CIC. Indeed, its annual level of sales, while more than $800 million in 1997, had been only $34 million as late as 1990. INEPAR has been particularly innovative in training, employee relations, and in management strategy. With respect to the latter, the firm has engaged in major searches for advanced technology, and entered into joint ventures with several leading U.S., European and Japanese firms. In addition to its purchases of Westinghouse and GE plants, the firm has expanded to sites to São Paulo, Rio de Janeiro and Buenos Aires, but its headquarters remains in Curitiba where nearly half of annual sales are generated. INEPAR boasted a highly productive workforce (which helped enable the enterprise to become the first in the city to qualify for the ISO 9000 standard), relatively low labor turnover and a low incidence of labor conflict. Another factor contributing to the decision to continue to center expansion plans in Curitiba has been the conviction of the enterprise leadership about the favorable Quality of Life of their native city. (Perhaps it should be noted that given INEPAR's concentration in the manufacture of telecommunications equipment, the company is doubtless much weaker at this time than just a few years back.)

Concluding Observations

Many factors contributed to the decisions to relocate to or reinvest in Curitiba during the period 1970-1998, but the active role of municipal (and, at times, state) authorities played a very significant role. The "Marketing of Curitiba" was extremely important in persuading those with plants in São Paulo or Rio (not to mention some firms still entirely abroad) to move to Paraná. Recent advances in the analysis of decision making by psychologists, economists and others help clarify why such a factor could be so important. The resulting boom in the city clearly motivated many young businessmen from Curitiba itself to change their way of thinking and launch more ambitious and risky undertakings than had been common among those from the area in the past. It is sometimes claimed that the changes in Curitiba gave a new sense of identity to the great majority of *curitibanos*; it certainty has been true for this group of entrepreneurs and they did not hesitate to say so. Did the Marketing of Curitiba also lead to a greater influx of unskilled job seekers than could be accommodated, and thus to an increase in unemployment and slum conditions greater than would otherwise have taken place? That is another matter, one that is not easy to answer, though something of the way in which the same municipal authorities have attempted to address the problems has already been touched upon and will be considered somewhat further in the closing chapter. One thing that is clear, in any event, is that the Curitiba experience clearly corresponds to Alexander Garvin's definition of urban planning as "…public action that will produce a substantial and widespread private market reaction." (Garvin in Le Gates and Stout 2000: 396)

---

[1] Seventy-nine interviews lasting one to three hours each were conducted by the author with 72 enterprises, government entities, or professionals. Of these, 34 were with producers, 33 from the private sector. This group included 8 foreign enterprises, most of which had established plants elsewhere in Brazil before coming to Curitiba, 1 Brazilian firm from São Paulo, 15 companies from the Curitiba area (8 of which had been established prior to 1970 and 7, subsequently), and 9 enterprises from other cities in the State of Paraná (Londrina and Maringá). With few exceptions, the interviews were conducted with the CEO or one of the leading members of the enterprise. A number of the professionals interviewed also had been prominent previously in private enterprises or in the government or both. Most of the enterprise interviews were facilitated by letters sent from the President of FIEP, José Carlos Gomes Carvalho, and follow-up phone calls by Maurilio Schmidt, Chief of the Economics Section, and economists Roberto Paredo and Daniel Fedato. Approximately half of the firms contacted agreed to participate. A progress report presented to the FIEP Board of Directors led to another interview. Sessions with two small firms were arranged with the assistance of Rosangela Maria

Angonese, the Director of the UNTAD sponsored EMPRETEC, which operated in cooperation with SEBRAE.

[2] Eakin 2001 makes the same observation with respect to Belo Horizonte and Minas Gerais.

[3] These assessments and those that follow cannot be taken fully at face value, particularly for the 1970s and 1980s, but they are helpful in understanding the surge of new investments undertaken in Curitiba, particularly since the respondents were encouraged to elaborate—to explain why the various factors were of consequence.

[4] A few prominent firms more closely related to agroindustry such as agricultural machinery producers did locate in the industrial park in the 1970s.

[5] A related note: Curitiba was beginning to become known as an excellent place in which to conduct market trials for new, middle- to upper-end consumer products.

[6] Although increased subcontracting has been a well-documented characteristic of increased efficiency throughout the world, detailed interviews with a number of Curitiba firms that made greater use of subcontracting raises questions about the degree to which the phenomenon increased the efficiency of manufacturing processes in those plants and the extent to which it contributed to lower product costs by lowering wages for those who became the subcontractors. Carleial 2001. Several efforts to help resolve this during the in-depth interviews undertaken for this study were inconclusive.

8

Conclusions: Lessons from the Past, Visions for the Future

Several visions circulate as to what Curitiba's image should be in the period ahead. The focus is no longer on the city alone, but on the Curitiba Metropolitan Region.

The first vision, that of the Lerner Group, is one of further industrial expansion in the context of socioeconomic concerns—a continuation of what has been one of the most distinguishing features of Curitiba's development over the last generation. Closely linked to that has been a concern, much as in the 1970s, to reduce unemployment. Both factors figured prominently in the mid-to-late 1990s campaigns to secure commitments from international producers of vehicles, leading to the establishment of assembly operations in Metropolitan Curitiba by Audi/Volkswagen, Renault/Nissan, and Daimler/Chrysler in addition to the previously established Volvo plant. As of 2000, both of these considerations showed preliminary signs of success. Another objective of the Lerner Group is to improve basic living conditions of those residing beyond the city's borders. The aim may be more modest than the Quality of Life aspirations originally espoused for Curitiba itself (and claimed to have been achieved by the 1990s) and does not appear to include the construction of the dramatic civic structures and international-stature public parks that have characterized Curitiba's rise to prominence. The explanation for the more modest objective derives not only from current budgetary considerations, but also from the reality that the population of the suburbs is not nearly as middle class as Curitiba itself and the infrastructure shortcomings are greater than they were within the city limits of Curitiba at the outset of the major changes there. Related to that, the Lerner Group has taken many of the concerns voiced by critics into account. Finally, there has been an effort by the city and also the State of Paraná to consolidate Curitiba as a Center for Innovation in Eco-Technology.

Other political groups have alternative visions for Curitiba, but if there is an overriding theme among them, it is that of getting the community to extend more attention to those in the most precarious socioeconomic situations, and to lower income individuals generally. This goal is combined with another, a concern for environmental matters that may be more like early manifestations of the Lerner Group than either the earlier position of those very same critics, or the current position of the Lerner associates. What seems to be missing in the approach of those opposing the Lerner Group, however, is any clear notion of how to provide a major new engine of continued growth that would provide the jobs and the financial resources to accommodate the socioeconomic objectives which they proclaim to seek.

Does what is presented in this report amount to anything more than a rendition of a particularly successful municipal experience that was a consequence of being in the right place at the right time almost as much as the positive contributions of urban planners and administrators with undeniable capability in marketing? Does it provide any indications of how to proceed with urban or other socioeconomic development elsewhere or even how to continue the process in Curitiba?

There are no laboratory tests of what has transpired nor any field tests drawing on the data that are available. Moreover, most of the principal actors have avoided explaining how they arrived at decisions, and, with rare exceptions, they have not allowed outsiders to observe them while they were in the process of making decisions.

Fortunately, that is not the end of the story.

There is a largely affirmative component to the answer, and this can be seen in part in the increasing number of cities that are in the process of adopting some of what has taken place in Curitiba, both in Brazil and abroad, especially in adapting Curitiba's approach to public transportation to their own situations.

The first lesson from the Curitiba experience is this: In any context with multiple objectives, the kind of global optimization that traditional economic analysis has assumed is desirable, simply is not feasible, and the constrained optimization or careful calculation of tradeoffs between the objectives found in much urban planning theory probably is not the most important consideration, even where it is feasible. Successful politicians and community leaders recognize this.

Some "second best" approach is required to proceed with urban renewal. It is advantageous to begin with a developmentally oriented, easily communicated vision. Jaime Lerner was extraordinarily adept at this. Not the most powerful speaker in a large group, he was, nonetheless, able to gain and hold the attention of audiences by drawing on materials that were readily accessible to sketch plausible new options that really had not been considered and that stirred the imagination of those to whom he spoke. The visions that are set forth in such exercises of urban renewal may be influenced by the concepts of urban planning or by other socioeconomic criteria. They must be coupled with well-identified objectives, however, and those objectives should remain consistent over a considerable stretch of time.

Second, it is important to get right to the business of implementation; quick implementation of what may be second best is likely to be more successful than that which is more fully conceived but overly delayed. In large measure this is because situations change and with them, what is optimal or even second best.

Third, some of the individuals who have the visions and set forth the objectives should become involved with the implementation of those objectives.

Fourth, since effective implementation is vital and often is much more difficult to work out than most social scientists imagine, it should not be left *entirely* to those with the initial visions, whose *forte*, alas, is rarely in implementation. Those who draw up the plans and initiate the process of urban revitalization should not leave the scene but they do need to be accompanied by others of a highly practical bent.

Fifth, the process of on-going implementation should be well documented. This is *especially* true since rarely will it be possible to proceed in an entirely systematic manner, with a continuing, clear view of tradeoffs and an estimate of the impact of what is being attempted. Documentation of what has taken place while it is occurring or very shortly thereafter reduces the likelihood of distortion and facilitates subsequent evaluation. Even those who achieved such successes as in Curitiba should consider this more carefully in their next moves. It is only then, at the very micro level, that a full-fledged effort to incorporate optimization calculations should take hold.

One lesson from all this, then, is that we should not begin to tackle practical problems of policy implementation with an excessively analytical, and "general equilibrium" approach, but we should try to keep such considerations in mind as implementation proceeds, perhaps assigning to some members of the urban renewal team, the responsibility of periodically reminding the others of those considerations. Start with visions capable of capturing the imagination of people and enlisting the efforts of those who seem to have a knack for getting things done and making things work. (Don't begin with elaborate plans.) If one can figure out workable principles of implementation (or at least catch serious mistakes along the way), all the better. Optimization techniques which enable the most to be made of available resources may be a *component* of such approaches, but only if they are deployed in conjunction with an understanding of likely psychological, sociological and cultural responses, and don't refer solely to technical considerations. If those who are successful in implementation cannot explain or perhaps even decipher the principles of their own success, don't get in their way by imposing elaborate justification requirements and procedural constraints at each step of the way. Rather, gather data about the decision-making processes *and the contexts in which the decisions are made.* That may aid in determining where such Rules of Thumb seem to work and where the heuristic approaches might advantageously be repeated as well as how improvements might be made to those approaches in the future. Strive for "second-best" and hope that the lessons learned along the way contribute to a more rational *process* of decision making and a better end result.

Such a set of guidelines may not be nearly as good as what we would like to have (and may one day succeed in designing), but the implications of such guidelines for successful urban planning and socioeconomic development are quite positive. One of the implications, even for Curitiba, is not only to move ahead in the manner just outlined, but, while there is still time, to try to elicit from those who were involved in the restructuring of the city, more about the reasoning underlying what they have done at the various stages. This will not be easy, given the inevitable biases involved in recall. It would entail a considerable rewriting of the interesting but very incomplete volumes of remembrances about the remaking of Curitiba that are available. It will be difficult to coax this out of the participants, of course, given the likelihood that political opponents will doubtless attempt to take advantage of any acknowledgements of chips in the armor. It would also be desirable to obtain something comparably candid from critics of Curitiba's process of urban change. That may be even harder to attain inasmuch as history may not seem to support some of the positions that they took, and those involved may first be gaining the opportunity to govern and may thus be reticent to do anything to undermine their chances of charting new courses. Finally, it would be desirable to learn more about the decision-making processes of the business community as well. While the latter may well be more willing to provide that information *ex post* than political leaders, they may be hard pressed to recall critical steps along the way since more of their decisions will have been taken quickly and not recorded.

Fuller explanation of municipal decision making in the past and continued attention to the reasoning processes underlying decision making for the period ahead is what is called for. That, accompanied by a further opening-up of the sessions of key deliberative bodies such as IPPUC, would constitute the real legacy that Curitiba has to offer the world about urban renewal and municipal revitalization. What is particularly and urgently required (and is so often overlooked in the academic community, perhaps understandably) is material that contributes to the critical but relatively unglamorous process of implementing development visions. Even if we are not yet ready for a theory of implementation, it is to be hoped that some useful suggestions can be drawn from the Curitiba experience and that those who have been a part of that process will help in providing still better guidelines of how to go about the implementation of urban renewal in the future.

Appendix A

Rules of Thumb
(Judgmental Heuristics)

Most of the important decisions in Curitiba's successful urban restructuring did not involve comprehensive optimization calculations. Rather, they reflected the use of rules of thumb—judgmental heuristics—that were modified over time and whose biases were increasingly recognized and taken into account during the process of implementation. The text refers to one of these, Anchoring and Adjustment, but various others also must have been employed. This appendix, modifies a summary on heuristics presented in the author's earlier overview of decision making and also reflects subsequent analyses on this topic.[1]

Many decisions are made without the benefit of carefully optimizing calculations, or they are made by combining optimizing techniques with various mental shortcuts. The latter sometimes dominate the results but the process may nonetheless often be characterized as a rational one, or at worst, as quasi-rational. The use of such heuristics is a response that takes account of the limited cognitive capacity to resolve problems, and is an effort to simplify the decision making process. It is often quite efficient to proceed in such a manner for minor or routine matters and it is sometimes necessary to do so when the situations are more complex. Decision makers use judgmental heuristics for many reasons.

To begin with, decision makers may be unaware of the best ways to solve many of the problems that confront them even when there is clearly a best way, and they may not have the time to determine these optimal solutions nor the resources to get others to help them, at least at a given point in time.

Second, optimization techniques may not have been devised for some types of problems. Indeed, some problems with multiple, somewhat conflicting objectives such as those of overall urban restructuring, may never lend themselves to unique, optimal solutions.

Third, a decision may be needed before extensive optimization calculations can be completed—though this is not quite as severe a problem as prior to recent advances in computer technology.

Fourth, the use of rules of thumb may enable a decision maker to keep certain matters secret until he or she chooses to make the decision known. Concern about this may offset the advances in computer technology and be of even greater importance in encouraging the use of rule-of-thumb alternatives to complete calculation than before, given the expanding activities of computer hackers and the new industrial piracy.

Fifth, use of a rule of thumb may be indicated because the decision maker may be unable to obtain all the information necessary for an optimizing solution, or the cost of obtaining the information may exceed the benefits added by moving toward an "optimizing" solution.

Sixth, the problem may not be so much in obtaining the information as in perceiving it accurately by the time the decision has to be made. Recall of past experiences may enable the decision maker to recognize this.

Seventh, an extraordinarily large amount of information may overwhelm the decision maker, not only because of the lack of (or unfamiliarity with) programs to handle the data, but also because of the emotional character of the particular decision (or the decision maker), the emotionally charged formulation of some data, or the state of awareness of the decision maker. (Consider, for example, the limitations of an artillery officer in calculating battery fire in the midst of a land and air siege, the difficulties of a police officer or a fireman during an urban riot or 9/11 type catastrophe, or the problems confronting a doctor or nurse faced with on-going emergencies over a twelve to eighteen hour tour of duty.) In all of these situations, affective, emotional and state of consciousness considerations may contribute to the justification of judgmental heuristics. Indeed, the latter may dominate the situation, and heuristics based on affect or emotion play more important roles than cognitive heuristics (or they may be critical in triggering certain cognitive heuristics). These are particularly important in certain consumer behavior and in many decisions beyond the realm of profit-oriented considerations.

Eighth, decision makers who ordinarily make optimization calculations may be tempted to stray from that course by rules of thumb that appear to be the "winning formulas" of others but which only *seem* to be more successful approaches or which, though more profitable, are characterized by higher risks and thus are not necessarily warranted by rational considerations.

Ninth, even where there is but a single objective and that objective is to optimize (as might be true for some specific, technical aspect of urban restructuring), the use of heuristics may be advisable if implementation of that objective presents serious difficulties for any reason—and even if only temporarily.

Most organizations have Standard Operating Procedures—SOPs. These are, in effect, rules of thumb or judgmental heuristics to deal with everyday situations and a few major types of decisions that are specific to the industry, firm or entity. Some SOPs are written and posted; others are learned over time or are implicit. Beyond that, individuals, enterprises and other organizations sometimes combine heuristics with detailed calculations in ways in which they have difficulty in explaining ex post. This sometimes leads to unwarranted use of the expression "reasoning by the seat of my pants" when what is really involved is the rational (or quasi rational) use of what Charles Lindblom called an incrementalist approach that is difficult for the decision maker to specify in any reasonably complete form.

Many in the social sciences have considered the possibility of generalizing alternatives to maximization and optimization, with economists arriving at these efforts long after investigators in sociology and business administration. Psychologists and marketing specialists have devoted a great deal of effort to explaining alternative approaches to decision making by consumers. Among the decision rule categories they have employed are affect referral, linear compensatory decision rules, nonlinear decision rules, conjunctive decision rules, disjunctive decision rules, lexicographic decision rules, sequential elimination, the lexicographic semiorder decision rule and the additive-difference decision rule. Further explorations are underway to try to explain the role of affect in judgment and decision making, and added to all this are the efforts of sociologists and anthropologists as well as psychologists to deal with the decision making of families and other special affinity groups. Some specialists at the border of economics, psychology and business administration contend that a guiding principal of organizational operation is a form of altruism that has been characterized as "enlightened selfishness." (This has been met, in turn, by those who emphasize the overriding presence of opportunism.) There has been an explosion of efforts to deal with the way in which decisions are made, some of it characterized as an adaptive approach to bounded rationality, recently extending to complexity theory (which has involved mathematicians and physical scientists), and neuroeconomics, involving particularly biologists.

Some judgmental heuristics are short and simple. Others, like Herbert Simon's early heuristic for locating warehouses, are more complex. Simon and later, many others devoted a great deal of effort to developing more generalizable heuristics. They introduced "heuristic programming," computer programs that simulated some non-quantitative, non-formal procedures that people use to solve problems. These programs—early undertakings in artificial intelligence—attempted to represent the mental processes of humans in terms of computer programs. They emphasized experience and allowed for the modification of performance. Building on Simon's early work to describe the decision making process as one guided by aspiration levels (in which reaching an aspiration level was regarded as *satisficing*) is the work of Reinhard Selten in expounding an aspiration adaptation theory.

The psychologists Amos Tversky, Daniel Kahneman, Paul Slovic and their colleagues advanced the discussion a step further. On the basis of their understanding of human behavior, they posited that individuals employ certain generalized rules of thumb or heuristics and they conducted numerous laboratory experiments to verify their hypotheses. Those experiments also revealed the nature of the biases associated with the heuristics—biases that most psychologists did not think were easy to reduce, much less eliminate. Some of the results they obtained seemed to undermine basic axioms of economics, which led economists and business administration specialists to run their own experiments, giving more attention to incentives than the psychologists had. To their surprise, at least initially, most of the economists found strong support for the conclusion that even those with incentives to optimize, individuals tended to use procedures that were only quasi-rational in terms of final results. However, later researchers have shown that even if use of those procedures did not assure what economists term ex post— substantive—rationality they possess the potential for being part of a rational *process* of decision making (provided that steps are taken to document the heuristics and to attempt to improve them or at least to take their biases into account). A number of laboratory experiments have revealed that individuals are able to reduce (even eliminate) the biases of their reasoning and move closer to what economists have termed rationality when presented with repeated, identical decisions. The jury is still out on the degree to which this learning carries over to experiments that are only similar (not identical) or that are repeated only after major lapses in time.

The emphasis, particularly by the psychologists, was initially on three heuristics: Representativeness, Availability, and Anchoring and Adjustment. The case for the generalized heuristics rests on these three and, to a lesser extent, on the matching law and melioration. <u>Representativeness</u>. Judgments of the likelihood of an event or an identification may be based on its similarity to a class of events or a group of characteristics. This kind of stereotyping often leads people to ignore even contrary probability data. (In one famous experiment, participants concluded that a sizable proportion of those in a small, seemingly random sample were librarians because those of the group they interviewed appeared to possess certain attributes that were often associated with people in that profession. The judgment was made despite the fact that the participants were provided with information in advance, indicating that the percentage of librarians in the base group was much lower.) Representativeness involves a statistically invalid reliance on small samples (the "law of small numbers"), a failure to allow for reversion to the mean (to allow for the fact that so-called "hot streaks" may be just that and not indications of new expected mean values), and reasoning by analogy, according to which judgments are based on the similarity, or seeming similarity of a situation to one that was faced before. <u>Availability (and availability cascades)</u>. A recall and consideration of certain information—dramatic or well publicized information or information particularly affecting the individual or entity in question—out of proportion to its statistical relevance. <u>Anchoring and Adjustment</u>. The overweighting of starting points such as recent historical data or numbers mentioned by first respondents irrespective of their reasonableness. <u>The Matching Law and Melioration</u>. The matching law refers to the tendency (particularly of animals, but also of humans in experimental situations) to equalize average (rather than marginal) rates of returns from competing alternatives. The shift toward the alternative that yields the better average rate of return is referred to as melioration.

Among other specific heuristics noted early-on are: Concreteness, Event Matching, Imitation, Simulation and Satisficing (where satisficing is combined with aspiration levels). Concreteness draws on the fact that people tend to remember information in the precise form that it is given to them. Event Matching is a procedure whereby people match their behavior to the properties of rewarded trials. (An example is in the approach of riders to catching a bus. If the bus arrives late one-third of the time, then while it might seem rational to always be at the bus stop on time, an event matching strategy would be to do so only two-thirds of the time.) Imitation has something in common with reasoning by analogy. The heuristic of Simulation uses as a basis for judgment, the ease with which examples or scenarios can be reconstructed. (It differs somewhat from what economists generally mean when they refer to the term.) Several heuristics that have received attention recently are Equal Weighting, Elimination by Aspects, Take-the-Best, Quick-Est, Which Feels Best?, Lex, and the aforementioned, Imitation. Recent work tends to show that the most important heuristics in everyday activity are quite context (domain) specific. Related to this is the conclusion of one prominent practitioner that what is required for many types of problem solving is a "progressive deepening" that reflects increasing expertise.

There are a number of problems, however. While these heuristics have been derived from the findings of psychology and it has been possible to ascertain the kinds of behavior exemplified by such heuristics as representativeness, availability, anchoring and adjustment, matching and melioration (and a large number of context specific heuristics), there is not yet any *theory* of heuristics. To date, the only general agreement seems to be that models of bounded rationality (for which heuristics can serve as a means of rational decision making) must incorporate simple rules for search, stopping that search and the actual making of decisions. The applicability of the various heuristics and the seriousness of the biases varies. Note that many psychologists and other workers in the area of bounded rationality believe that it is possible to identify other important heuristics by careful questioning and observation in real-life situations. Many problems apparently draw on more than a single heuristic, but to date, there are no guidelines for anticipating the mix of heuristics that may apply to different types of problems or the degree to which the biases detected for the various heuristics may be altered when they are combined (or when they are used in any particular sequence) or if they vary according to external circumstances or the emotional state of the decision maker. Views on the significance of heuristics are beginning to be influenced by new findings regarding the role of affect on judgment and decision making. More generally, the framing of information seems to influence the heuristics that are relevant and the extent of their relevance.

Decision makers use rules of thumb (judgmental heuristics) and we know more about them than before, but how many heuristics with which types and degrees of bias may be at work in resolving the often complex problems of individuals, businesses and government? How do the sometimes only quasi-rational heuristics of highly successful survivors (and the way in which those heuristics are improved or at least their biases are detected) differ from those of businesses that barely get by, consumers who don't seem to have as high standard of living as others with comparable levels of income, and municipalities that seem to be deteriorating? Case studies of at least moderately complicated field situations and studies involving interviews of decision makers are underway and such inductive efforts may be the key to uncovering a theory of survivor-oriented heuristics and a prescriptive theory of socioeconomics.

---

[1]   See Appendix A in Schwartz 1998, Schwartz 2003, Gigerenzer and Selten 2002, Slovic et al 2002 and Frank 2003.

Appendix B

Jaime Lerner: A Brief Biography[1]

Three times mayor, twice governor, Jaime Lerner, the man most associated with making Curitiba, Brazil a synonym for a modern and highly livable urban metropolis, was born in 1937. Lerner graduated as an architect and urban planner from the School of Architecture of the Federal University of Paraná in 1964. He participated as part of the local counterpart in drawing up the *Master Plan* (*Guidelines*) that was presented in 1965-66 and which led to the physical, economic and cultural transformation of the City of Curitiba. Lerner was the key figure in the formation of IPPUC, the Institute of Urban Planning and Research of Curitiba, working in the institute from 1966-71 and serving as Director during 1968-69.

In 1971, Jaime Lerner, a 33-year-old technician not then politically active, was designated Mayor of Curitiba. He was re-appointed in 1979. When he finished that term of office a survey of the Brazilian Institute of Opinion Polls and Statistics named him as the most popular mayor in the country. Later, in 1989, he was elected for a third term. Lerner had run for mayor at the start of the new series of municipal elections in 1986, but lost on that occasion to Roberto Requião, another popular political figure. Lerner was elected governor in 1994, and when he ran for a second term in 1998, he defeated Requião.

During his first term as mayor, Lerner led the city in a municipal rejuvenation that included the transformation of downtown, converting five blocks of the most important commercial thoroughfare of the city into a major pedestrian mall—though not without controversy. He presided over the initiation of an industrial park larger and greener than in any other city in the world and the establishment of an integrated mass transport system with unique features that avoided concentration on downtown and became known for its efficiency and low cost.

Lerner was followed in office by a close associate who continued the programs that Lerner had begun. When he returned for a second term in 1979, he continued work on the transport system, establishing a single fare system that subsidized travel from outlying parts of the city where most of those with lower incomes lived. The reelected mayor also extended added attention to parks and public forests, which advanced recreational objectives while better managing flood control. In his third term in office, further innovations were introduced to public transport, establishing Curitiba as an international model for medium size cities. The space dedicated to public parks and forests expanded to twenty times more per city resident than in 1970 (considerably more than that by some accounts), even as the city's population tripled. Ecological objectives were pursued along with a number of projects for the beautification of Curitiba and living standards were improved. The latter included not only basic socioeconomic infrastructure and services but also increased attention to safety net features for lower income individuals, some of which he had initiated in his previous administrations and others of which had been initiated by the opposition administrations during the 1980s.

Elected Governor of Paraná in 1994, Lerner extended his visionary concepts to the state and, with international assistance, endeavored to replicate some of the infrastructure projects that had proven so successful in Curitiba. The social, educational and child care achievements led to Paraná's receiving the Child and Peace Award from UNICEF in 1996. In addition, Governor Lerner energetically sought increased foreign investment for the state, and succeeded in attracting $20 billion to Paraná between 1995 and 2001. Some questions were raised about the way this was achieved, as noted in the text, particularly by Roberto Requião, his long-time opponent.

Jaime Lerner and his associates began as a "technician group" though the Lerner Group, as they were usually referred to, soon became very much enmeshed in politics. The political associations of the Group shifted over time. Lerner's initial appointment as mayor came during the period of the military government. When municipal elections were reestablished in 1985 the Lerner Group affiliated with the populist-oriented party of Leonel Brizola. In 1995, with polls showing an 83% approval rating for Governor Lerner, a number of those in the party sought to have him replace Brizola as their candidate for president, but within a few years, Lerner advisors and close supporters attempted to have the governor affiliate with one of the principal centrist parties, if possible, that of President Fernando Henrique Cardoso, with whom Lerner was closely allied. When officials of the president's party in Paraná blocked that effort, Lerner and his associates were invited to join another party also allied with Cardoso, a more right wing group associated with the Magalhães family of Bahia that included the leaders of both houses of Congress.

When not in public office, Jaime Lerner has been actively engaged as an architect and urban planner, both in Brazil and beyond, on a number of occasions for the United Nations. He developed plans for more than half a dozen cities in Brazil and coordinated the Rio Year 2000 program that recommended guidelines for mass transport and revitalization of the inner city. Lerner participated in drawing up urban and mass transport plans for Caracas, Venezuela, San Juan, Puerto Rico, Shanghai, China and Havana, Cuba. Academically, he has been a Professor of Architecture and Urban Planning and Dean of the School of Architecture at the Federal University of Paraná, and was Regent Visiting Professor at the University of California at Berkeley.

In the 1960s Jaime Lerner and his team won two important awards in architectural contests, one in Brazil and a second in Spain. He was a member of the group of young architects representing Brazil at the Paris Biennial Exhibition in 1969. In 1989, he was awarded the Silver Medal at the International City Design Competition organized by the School of Architecture and Urban Planning of the University of Wisconsin, Milwaukee. Lerner has been a member of many Brazilian societies, the coordinator of the Commission on Human Settlements for Latin America and the Caribbean, and in 2002 was elected President of the International Union of Architects. The Jaime Lerner Institute, which the governor helped establish that same year, focuses on the dissemination of urban management strategies.

Programs promoted by Jaime Lerner have led to a good deal of international recognition for Curitiba. In 1990, the United Nations granted Curitiba awards for its programs, Garbage That Isn't Garbage, which emphasized the separation of garbage than can be recycled, and the Household Garbage Purchase program for collecting garbage from areas not accessible to large vehicles. In the same year Curitiba received the annual award of the International Institute for Energy Conservation for fostering energy conservation in overall city planning. Curitiba was included among 12 global cities singled out during the Earth Summit in Rio de Janeiro in 1992 and in 1995 the city was selected as the site for the United Nations Habitat I.

Jaime Lerner received the highest award of the United Nations Environmental Program in 1990, and in the same year he was honored with the award of the International Institute for Energy Conservation and with two awards for environmental conservation at Expo '90 in Osaka, Japan.

In 1991, he received honors from the International Union for Nature Conservation and the U.S. Worldwatch Institute. ECO '92 granted him special recognition, and in 1996 he was singled out, among others, by the Brazilian Sales Managers Association for his success in marketing. Lerner was awarded the Thomas Jefferson Medal from the University of Virginia in 1997. Further awards in the years 2000-2002 included recognition by Urban Heroes (The Netherlands), the International Council for Caring Communities (U.S.), The National Museum for Science and Industry (United Kingdom—the World Technology Award for Transportation), and the International Union of Architects for improvement in the quality of human settlements.

Jaime Lerner has participated in numerous international meetings and in this connection has delivered presentations at the Smithsonian Institution, the United Nations, the New York Academy of Sciences, the World Congress on Land Policy, the World Congress of Architects, Columbia University, New York University, the University of Cincinnati, and has given seminars in Colombia, Puerto Rico, Spain, Great Britain, Japan, the United States and China. He made one of the principal presentations to the International Forum on Sustainable Cities at The George Washington University in 2002. Lerner holds honorary doctorates from four universities and has received special recognition from the national institutes of architects in four countries.

With all of this, and however much he may have owed his original designation as mayor to the fact that he was a prominent technician in the field of urban planning, Jaime Lerner soon became and has long remained very much a political figure. Indeed, if he had not become heavily involved in politics it is difficult to imagine how he would have accomplished all that he has in transforming and revitalizing a very traditional community, and in stirring the interest of a national and then international audience—not just in the years immediately after publication of the *Guidelines*, but over the course of a generation.

---

[1] This brief biography draws on a number of sources, particularly notes sent by Paulo Krauss of the Jaime Lerner Institute. The views stated are those of the author and may not reflect those of Mr. Krauss or any of the other sources used.

Appendix C

Mayors of Curitiba, Governors of Paraná, 1964-2002

Mayors of Curitiba

1964-67: Ivo Arzua Pereira (1963-67)

1967-71: Omar Sabbag

1971: Edgar Dantas Pimental

1971-74: Jaime Lerner

1974: Donato Gulin

1975-79: Saul Raiz

1979-83: Jaime Lerner

1983-85: Maurício Fruet

1986-88: Roberto Requião de Mello e Silva

1989-92: Jaime Lerner

1993-96: Rafael Greca de Macedo

1997-2001: Cassio Taniguchi

elected in 2002: Cassio Taniguchi

Governors of Paraná

1964: Ney Braga (1960-64)

1965-71: Paulo Cruz Pimentel

1971: Haroldo Leon Peres

1971-73: Pedro Viriato Parigot de Souza

1973: João Mansur

1973-75: Emilio Hoffmann Gomes

1975-79: Jayme Canet Júnior

1979-82: Ney Braga

1983-86: José Richa

1987-90: Alvaro Dias

1991-94: Roberto Requião de Mello e Silva

1995-98: Jaime Lerner

1999-2002: Jaime Lerner

Glossary and Guide to Acronyms

Anchoring and Adjustment: A heuristic or Rule of Thumb that involves adjustment from a given point such as recent historical data or an existing pattern of development rather than comprehensive calculation on the basis of all relevant information. See also, heuristic, below, and Appendix A, Rules of Thumb.

BADEP: Development Bank of Paraná (established in 1968, closed in 1987).

BNDES: National Bank for Economic and Social Development.

CEFET: Brazil's leading secondary-through-post secondary technical training institute.

CIC: Industrial City of Curitiba (later, Curitiba Development Company).

CODEPAR: Development Company of Paraná (established in 1961, transformed into BADEP in 1968).

COMEC: Curitiba Region Coordination Council.

Constrained optimization: Optimization (see below) after taking account of one or more specific factors that limit (constrain) the ability to obtain the best result possible (a fully optimal result).

COPEL: Electric Power Company of Brazil.

Economic rationality: the process of attempting to obtain the greatest gain possible in economic terms; the attempt to pursue maximization (optimization).

EMPRETEC: A capacity building program of UNCTAD, the United Nations Trade and Development Organization, aimed at fostering the growth and competitiveness of small and medium scale enterprise in developing countries, based in large measure on the concepts of social psychologist David McClelland.

FDE: Economic Development Fund.

FIEP: Federation of Industries of Paraná.

General equilibrium approach: an approach that reveals the economic impact after allowing for the effects of all factors, large and small, and that takes account of the consequences of each factor on all others.

Heuristic, judgmental heuristic: any principle, rule of thumb or technique that reduces what is required to solve a problem; a short cut that facilitates problem solving (though one which, because of the incomplete inclusion of information and/or calculation, is usually characterized by biases). See Appendix A, Rules of Thumb.

Implicit discount rate: A discount rate is the rate at which future streams of income or profits are reduced to arrive at their present value or their value at a given point in time, ordinarily reflecting the rate of return to capital in the economy. The implicit discount rate referred to in this book is the presumably low rate of discount of future income or profits that would have been necessary to justify the infrastructure expenditures used to prepare the Industrial City of Curitiba at the time they were undertaken in the 1970s.

Incrementalism, "muddling through": an approach to implementation that reflects a continuing reassessment of the situation and the selection of alternatives determined by the prevailing circumstances and context rather than any long term plan or design. The major expositions of the concept are those of the economist/political scientist Charles Lindblom.

IPARDES: Institute of Economic and Social Development (of the State Government of Paraná).

IPUCC: Research and Planning Institute of Curitiba.

Maximization: see Optimization.

MERCOSUL, MERCOSUR: Common Market Integration Agreement of Brazil, Argentina, Uruguay and Paraguay.

Negative real rates of interest: interest at rates less than the rate of inflation. Negative real rates of interest lead to loan repayment obligations lower in terms of purchasing power than the original amount of the loan, and thus, a subsidy to the borrower. (Some subsidy is involved if interest rates are lower than those that would be called for in economic terms even if the real rates of interest are not quite so low as to reach negative levels.)

Optimization techniques: techniques that facilitate calculation of results that are optimal in economic terms.

Optimization, global optimization: the process of combining resources in the manner that yields the greatest possible economic outcome (the greatest possible economic return) or that attempts to do so; an effort to pursue economic rationality to the fullest.

RMC: Curitiba Metropolitan Region.

SEBRAE: Brazil's national agency that provides technical assistance for small and medium enterprise.

SENAI: Brazil's national agency that provides training for workers and technicians.

Second-best approach: the best approach to employ—the approach that offers the best outcome possible—given the presence of market imperfections or other obstacles that make it impossible to optimize, i. e., to obtain fully optimal results.

SUDENE: Development Superintendency of the Northeast (Development Corporation of Northeast Brazil).

TECPAR: Technical Assistance Agency of the State of Paraná.

TELEPAR: Telephone Company of the State of Paraná.

UNICEF: United Nations Children's Fund

UNIDO: United Nations Industrial Development Organization

Urban planning theory:

> Functional urban planning theory: planning with the goals and objectives taken as given. (This is subject to the criticism of some urban planning authorities that there is no compelling functional theory—no agreement as to what goals and objectives should be taken into account.)

> Normative urban planning theory: planning theory in which the objectives are determined by the planner in a manner deemed to be rational in a sense that is clearly defined.

URBS: Urbanization Company of Curitiba.

Bibliography

AECIC (Association of Enterprises of the Industrial City of Curitiba) *AECIC News* (1997-1998). Various issues.

Assad, Abrão Anis (1973). "Revitalizão de um Centro Urbano." *Revista de Arquitectura, Planejamento e Construção.* (September-October): 112-119.

Augusto, Maria Helena Oliva (1978). *Intervencionismo estatal e ideologia desenvolvimentista. Estudo sobre a CODEPAR.* São Paulo, Brazil: Símbolo.

Braga, Ney (1996). *Tradição e Mudança na Vida Política.* Entrevista a Adherbal Fortes de Sá Junior. Curitiba, Brazil: Viação Garcia.

Cámara Municipal, Curitiba (1997). Seminário Sobre O "Plano Diretor de 1965:" Transcripts of sessions of May-June 1997.

Campbell, Scott and Susan S. Fainstein (eds.) (1996). *Readings in Planning Theory.* Cambridge, MA and Oxford, UK.

Carleial, Liana M. F. (2001). *Redes Industriais de Subcontração: um Enfoque do Sistema Nacional de Inovações.* São Paulo, Brazil: Hucitec.

Carneiro Leáo, Igor Zanoni Constant (1989). *O Paraná nos Anos Setenta.* Curitiba, Brazil: IPARDES and Conselho de Ciéncia e Tecnologia.

Castro, Demian (July 1997). *Aspectos da Guerra Fiscal no Brasil: A Política de Incentivos Fiscais no Paraná.* Curitiba, Brazil: Fundação do Desenvolvimento Administrativo.

Ceneviva, Carlos [n.d. 1999?]. Curitiba e sua Rede Integrada de Transporte. Curitiba, Brazil. Manuscript.

CIC (Industrial City of Curitiba) (1995) "How to Establish Company Policy in an Ethical and Efficient Way." Curitiba, Brazil. Manuscript of lecture by Maria Elisa Ferraz Paciornik.

CNI (Confederação Nacional de Indústria) (1994-1998) *Indústria e Productividade.* Various issues.

Da Cunha, Sieglinde Kindl (1995). *Política Científica e Tecnológica: Novas Trajectórias Institucionais para o Estado do Paraná.* Ph.D. dissertation, Department of Economics, State University of Campinas. Campinas, Brazil.

Deconto, Vilson and Carlos De Carlos Stoltze, *Formação de uma estratégia governamental* (1982). Curitiba, Brazil: Secretaria de Estado da Cultura e do Esporte.

Del Santoro, Roberto D. V. (2000). Curitiba. A Evolução Ao Sucesso. Curitiba, Brazil: PARANÁCIDADE. Manuscript.

Desenvolvimento Empresarial (1977). Various issues.

Direção. (1997). Various issues.

Divulgação Paraná (1995-97). Various issues.

Eakin, Marshall C. (2001). *Tropical Capitalism. The Industrialization of Belo Horizonte, Brazil.* New York and Hampshire, England: Palgrave.

Economic Commission for Latin America and the Caribbean, Joint Unit on Transnational Corporations (1993) *Transnational Corporations and the Manufacturing Sector in Brazil.* Manuscript reproduced without formal editing.

The Economist (1996). "Off the rails." June 22: 15.

Embajada Argentina en Brasil (1995). *Argentina-Brasil. Comercio, Inversiones e Integración Física.*

Estado de São Paulo (1996) *Law No. 9,262, July 24, 1996.*

Expressão Paraná (1997). Various issues.

Fachini, Justino (1975). *A Significação Social do Planejamento Urbano. Estudo do Caso de Curitiba.* Master's Thesis, Department of Urbanism, School of Architecture, Federal University of Rio Grande do Sul. Porto Alegre, Brazil. The first major effort to evaluate the early stages of urban redevelopment in Curitiba.

FIEP (Federação das Industrias do Estado do Paraná) (1985-1997). *Sistema de Indicadores Conjunturais da Indústria do Estado do Paraná.* Various issues.

_____, Departamento Econômico (n.d.). *Economia Paranaense. Sinopse Industrial: 1994.* Curitiba, Brazil.

Frank, Robert H. (2003). "Departures from Rational Choice: With and Without Regret." Presentation to Biennial Meeting, Society for the Advancement of Behavioral Economics, Lake Tahoe, Nevada, July 28-31, 2003.

Gazeta do Povo (1995-2001). Various issues.

Gigerenzer, Gerd and Reinhard Selten (eds.) (2001). *Bounded Rationality. The Adaptive Toolbox.* Cambridge, MA and London, England: The MIT Press.

Governo Fernando Henrique Cardoso [n. d. 1994?]. *Política Industrial, Tecnológica e de Comércio Exterior. Reestructuração e Expansão Competitivas do Sistema Industrial Brasileiro, 1995-1999.* Brasilia. Brazil.

Governo do Estado Paraná [n. d. 1995?]. *Programa Paraná Mais Empregos. Plano de Desenvolvimento do Paraná.* Curitiba, Brazil.

_____ (n. d. 1995?]. *Plano de Governo.* Curitiba, Brazil.

_____ (1997). *Jaime Lerner, Relato das Principais Ações e Programas de 1996. Mensagem de 1997 a Assembléia Legislativa.* Curitiba, Brazil.

_____, Secretaria de Estado da Indústria, do Comercio e do Desenvolvimento Econômico do Paraná (1996). *Sonagem Industrial II. A Visão de Lideres Industriais Paranaenses, 1996-1997.* Curitiba, Brazil.

_____, Secretaria do Planejamento e Coordenação Geral, Secretaria da Indústria, Comercio e Desenvolvimento Econômico (1996). *Relatorio de Atividades, Janeiro 1995/Maio 1996* (Cassio Taniguchi). Curitiba, Brazil.

Greca de Macedo, Rafael [n.d. 1995?]. Curitiba, Igualdade de Oportunidades. Curitiba, Brazil. Manuscript of speech.

Guimarães Gouvea, Ronaldo (2001). "Autonomia Municipal em Regiões Metropolitanas: As Questões Administrativa e Política." Presentation to the XXIII International Congress of Latin American Studies Association, LASA 2001 Washington, DC, September 13-15, 2001.

Hawken, Paul, Amory and L. Hunter Lovens (1999). *Natural Capitalism. Creating the Next Industrial Revolution.* New York: Little, Brown and Co. Most of Chapter 14, "Human Capitalism," deals with Curitiba (Weaving the Web of Solution: The Curitiba Example).

Hiroshi Yoshizawa, Luiz (1979?). Perfil das Empresas do Estado do Paraná. Curitiba, Brazil. Manuscript.

Idéia (1997). Various issues.

INEPAR (1991) *Practical Results in Quality and Production Cultural Modifications.* Curitiba, Brazil.

Instituto Brasileiro de Qualidade e Produtividade-Paraná (1998). *Productividade nas Empresas Paranaenses – Pesquisa Básica.* Curitiba, Brazil: Summary from website.

142 • URBAN RENEWAL, MUNICIPAL REVITALIZATION

IPARDES (Paraná Institute of Economic and Social Development) (1967-82; 1995-98). *A Revista Paranaense de Desenvolvimento.* Various issues.

_____ (1974 and 1975). *Estudo de Integração de Polos Agro-Indústriais do Paraná.* 3 vols. Curitiba, Brazil.

_____ (1975). *Programa de Agro-Indústria do Estado do Paraná.* Curitiba, Brazil.

_____ (1978). *A Contribução da CODEPAR e BADEP para o Financiamento do Desenvolvimento da Economia Paranaense.* Curitiba, Brazil.

_____ (1980). *Estudo dos Fatores de Decisão na Implantação de Indústrias na Região Metropolitana de Curitiba.* Curitiba, Brazil.

_____ (1981). *Estudos para uma Política de Desenvolvimento Industrial no Paraná.* 4 vols. Curitiba, Brazil.

_____ (1982). *Paraná:Economia e Sociedade.* Curitiba, Brazil.4 volumes. Curitiba, Brazil. Vol. I: *A Desconcentração Industrial e as Perspectivas do Paraná;* Vol. II: *Avaliação dos Distritos Indústriais e Potencialidades Municipais;* Vol. III: *Instrumentos Estaduais de Apoio á Indústria;* Vol. IV: *Distribução Espacial da Indústria Paranaense.*

_____ (1987). *Elementos para uma Política de Desenvolvimento Urbano para o Paraná.* Curitiba, Brazil.

_____ (1993). *Boletim de Análise Conjuntural: textos selecionados.* Curitiba, Brazil.

_____ (1989-2000). *Análise Conjuntural.* Various issues.

_____ (1994). *Temas Estratégicos para o Paraná.* Curitiba, Brazil.

_____ (1994). Competitividade da Indústria Paranaense: Uma Análise Setorial. Curitiba, Brazil.

_____ and Conselho de Desenvolvimento da Região Sul (CODESUL) (1980). *Estudo dos Fatores de Decisão na implantacão de Industrias na Região de Curitiba.* Curitiba, Brazil.

_____ (1997). *Perfil do Setor de Informática em Curitiba 95/96.* Curitiba, Brazil

IPPUC (Curitiba Research and Urban Planning Institute) (1966). Plano Diretor. (Lei No.2.8281.66). Curitiba, Brazil.

_____ (1978?). *Curitiba. Uma experiencia de planejamento urbano.* Curitiba, Brazil.

_____ (1986?). *20 anos planejando Curitiba con voce.* Curitiba, Brazil.

_____ (1989-91). *Memória da Curitiba Urbana.* 7 volumes. Curitiba, Brazil. Reflections on the process of urban redevelopment of Curitiba. Indispensable for understanding recent development in the city though lacking in details about the actual decision making process. Vol. 1 (1989) is the statement of Ivo Arzua Pereira, Mayor at the time of the preparation of the "Master Plan" in 1965-66. Vol. 2 (1990) contains statements by Clóvis Lunardi, Rafael Dely and Carlos Eduardo Ceneviva and an outline of the development of the city's bus system. Vol. 3, (1990, reissued in 1992) contains statements by Francisca M. G. Rischbieter, Lubomir Ficinski Dunin, Nicolau Imthon Klüppel, Angel Walter Bernal and Cassio Taniguchi. Vol. 4 (1990, reissued in 1992) contains statements by Dúlcia Auríquio, Alberto M. Da Rocha Paranhos, Abrão Assad, Rafael V. Greca de Macedo, two university professors and several journalists. Vol. 5 (1990) contains statements by Ney Aminthas de Barros Braga, Karlos Rischbieter, Jorge Wilheim, Onaldo Pinto de Oliveira, Saul Raiz, Euclides Rovani, Mário Gomes de Mello Leitão Filho and several journalists as well as a list of all of the publications of IPPUC through the date publication of this volume of remembrances. Vol. 6 (1991) is focused on the Industrial City of Curitiba and contains statements by Eduardo Sganzerla, Emílio Hoffman Gomes, Karlos Heinz Rischbieter. Cassio Taniguchi, João Mansur, Renato Antônio Johnsson, Arturo Andreoli, Luis Antonio Fayet, Kanitar Aymoré Sabóia Cordeiro, Francisco Ernesto Alves Macedo, Luiz Groff, Rubens Jacob Teig, Dario Lopes dos Santos, Aldo Almeida Júnior, Mario Busato, Ivens Moretti Pacheco, Luiz Albuquerque Beatrice, Martinho Faust, Atilano Oms Sobrinho, Leo Roberto Diedrich, Hogdan Bembnowski, Hilton Dacio Trevisan, Ofélia de Jesus Gomes, Júnior Paulo Vieira, Giovani Gionédis, Celso Nascimento, as well as a brief account of the establishment of Ford New Holland, a description of the SENAI/CIC training center, and a year-by-year list of the enterprises that established themselves in the industrial city. Vol. 7 (1991) deals with the concept and practice of urban planning and contains statements by Euro Brandão, Theodócio Jorge Atherino, Almir Fernándes, Luiz Forte Netto, Gustavo Gama Monteiro, Marlene Fernandes, José Maria Valduga, Auner Pereira Carneiro, Alfred Willer, Constatino Batista Viaro, Ennio Marques Ferreira, Maria Elisa Ferraz Paciornik, Lidia Maria Bindo Dely, Manoel Coelho, Omar Akel, Luiz Masaru Hayakawa, Nereu Barão,

Zélia Passos, Osvaldo Navarro Alves, Maria José Malucelli, Eloy Silvestre Kochanny, Lauro Tomizawa, Milna Oliveira Leone, Flávio D'Aquino, and Frei Miguel Botacin.
_____ (1992). *Memória da Curitiba Urbana*. Edition Speciale. Ecole D'Urbanisme Ecologique. Curitiba, Brazil.
_____ (1995). *Planejamento Urbano*. Curitiba, Brazil.
_____ (1995). *Circulação Viária: Estágio Aplicado em Gestão Urbana*. Curitiba, Brazil.
_____ (1995). *Controle de Tráfego em Area. Estágio Aplicado em Gestão Urbana*. Curitiba, Brazil.
_____ (1995). *Geoprocessamento. Estágio Aplicado em Gestão Urbana*. Curitiba, Brazil.
_____ (1995). *Planejamento Sócio-Econômico. Estágio Aplicado em Gestão Urbana*. Curitiba, Brazil.
_____ (1996). *Curitiba. Uma experiencia de planificação*.Curitiba, Brazil.
_____ (1996). *Planejamento Socio-Econômico*. Curitiba, Brazil.
_____ (1996). *Qualidade de Vida em Curitiba*. Curitiba, Brazil.
_____ and IPEA (Institute of Economic Research) (1997). *Monitoração da Gestão Urbana. Gestão do uso de solo e disfunções do crecimento urbano da região Metropolitana de Curitiba*. Curitiba, Brazil.
Journal da FIEP (Federation of Industries of the State of Paraná) (1997). Various issues.
Journal da Industria & Comércio do Paraná (1995, 1997, 1998). Various issues.
_____ (1995). *Paraná Export. Export Directory of the State of Paraná. Brazil 1995*. Curitiba, Brazil.
Kapaz, Emerson (July 1997). *Estratégia Competitiva do Estado*. São Paulo, Brazil.
Kepp, Michael (1996?), "Paraná Infrastructure." *Infrastructure Finance*.
Kleindorfer, Paul R., Howard C. Kunreuther and Paul J. H. Schoemaker (1993). *Decision Sciences: An Integrative Perspective*. New York: Cambridge University Press. Ch. 9
Le Gates, Richard T. and Frederic Stout (eds). (2000). *The City Reader*. Second Edition. London and New York: Routledge.
Lerner, Jaime (1994). *Plano de Governo*. Curitiba, Brazil.
_____(2003). E-mail to Hugh Schwartz (Comments to manuscript, *Urban Renewal, Municipal Revitalization)*. October 9, 2003.

Lindblom, C. E. (1959). "The Science of Muddling Through." *Public Administration Review*. Vol. xix: 79-88.

Lowry, Ira S. (November 2002). *Municipal Development in Paraná. Policies and Programs, 1981-2001*. PARANACIDADE (Secretariat de Urban Development, State of Paraná), Curitiba, Paraná, Brazil. Study sponsored by the United Nations Development Program, UNDP Project BRA/95/005.

Magalhães Filho, Francisco de Borja Baptista (1972 & 1996). "Evolução histórica da economia paranaense." *A Revista Paranaense de Desenvolvimento* No.87 (January/April): 131-48.

_____ (1995). "Agentes sociais do Paraná." *A Revista Paranaense de Desenvolvimento* No.86 (September/December): 3-34.

_____(1997). *As Metróploes do notre paranaense*. UNDP Project BRA/95/005. Curitiba, Brazil.

Menezes, Claudino Luiz (1996). *Desenvolvimento Urbano e Meio Ambiente. A Experiência de Curitiba*. São Paulo, Brazil: Papirus Editora.

Meyer-Stamer, Jorg (1996). Filling the Local Space: Obstacles to Strengthening Industrial Competitiveness on the Local and Regional Level-The Case of Santa Catarina/Brazil. Paper prepared for EADI Conference, Vienna, 11-14 September.

Mills, Edwin S. (ed.) (1987). *Handbook of Regional and Urban Economics*. Vol. II. *Urban Economics*. Amsterdam: North-Holland.

_____ and Bruce W. Hamilton (1994). *Urban Economics*. Fifth Edition. New York: Harper Collins.

Municípios em Destaque (1997). *Edição Especial de Aniversário 304 anos. Curitiba 9/023/1997*. Curitiba, Brazil.

Nicholls, William H. (1969). "The Transformation of Agriculture in a Presently Semi-Industrialized Country: The Case of Brazil." In Erik Thorbeke, ed., *The Role of Agriculture in Economic Development*. A Conference of Universities-National Bureau of Economic Research Publication. Columbia University Press. New York and London: 311-78.

_____ and R. M. Paiva (May 1965). "The Structure and Productivity of Brazilian Agriculture." *Journal of Farm Economics*. Vol. 47: 347-61.

Oliveira, Dennison de (1997). "Empresários, burocratas e a formação de alianças políticas regionais: o Caso do 'Grupo de los 13' e dos 'Cinco Jotas.' Unpublished manuscript. Curitiba, Brazil.

_____ (2000). *Curitiba e o mito da cidade modelo*. Curitiba, Brazil: Editora UFPR. One of the most important references available on the recent urbanization of Curitiba, the best documented and most scholarly of the critical commentaries, while still quite readable. Even so, the book, basically a 1995 doctoral dissertation in history from the University of Campinas, contains material that is more inflammatory than would be expected from a dissertation. Dennison de Oliveira is Professor of History and former Chairman of the Department of History at the Federal University of Paraná in Curitiba.

Padis, Pedro Calil (1981). *Formação de uma economia periférica: o caso do Paraná*. São Paulo, Brazil: Editora Hucitee. Printed with the cooperation of the Secretary of Culture and Sports of the State of Paraná. Originally a 1970 doctoral dissertation of The Pontifical Catholic University of São Paulo.

Paraná (1992, also two others, n.d.). The State of Paraná, Brazil. Curitiba.

Paraná em Páginas (1997). Various issues.

Paraná-Urbano: Sustainable Urban Development (1998-1999). Various documents. Curitiba, Brazil.

Prefeitura Municipal de Curitiba, IPPUC (1965). *Plano Preliminar de Urbanismo de Curitiba*. Prepared by Sociedade Serete de Estudos e Projetos Ltda. and Jorge Wilheim, Arquitetos Associados for IPPUC, Curitiba's planning agency. Curitiba, Brazil.This is the draft of the "Master Plan" for the urban redevelopment of Curitiba.

_____, IPPUC (1966). *Plano Diretor*. Curitiba, Brazil. The Master Plan for urban redevelopment, approved July 31, 1966.

_____ (1996). *Curitiba*. Curitiba, Brazil. An official presentation of the history of the city with numerous photographs. Curitiba, Brazil.

_____, Department of Industry, Commerce and Tourism (1996, 1997). *Curitiba. Social and Economic Indicators*. Curitiba, Brazil.

_____ (n. d. 1997?). *Development with Quality of Life*. Curitiba, Brazil.

_____ (n. d. 1997?). *Software Park*. Curitiba, Brazil.

Quandt, Maria do Rocio Morais do Rosario (1985). *Urban Planning Practice: A Social Process, A Technical Exercise or a Political Action?: Evidence from the Curitiba Case Study in the Context of Brazilian Urban Politics*. Master's Thesis, Bastlett School of Architecture and Urban Planning, University College, London. A particularly useful reference for the period through 1982.

Rabinovitch, Jonas and Josef Leitman (1993). *Environmental Innovation and Management in Curitiba, Brazil.* UNDP/UNCHS (Habitat)/ The World Bank. Urban Management Program. Working Paper No. 1. Washington, D.C.

_____ (March 1996). "Urban Planning in Curitiba." *Scientific American.* Vol. 274, No. 3: 46-53.

Ribeiro, Luiz Carlos (1991). *Le Patronat et Les Pouvoirs Publics au Paraná (Brasil), 1940-1965.* Ph.D. Dissertation, Institute of Advanced Studies of Latin America, New University of the Sorbonne (III). Paris, France.

Sánchez Garcia, Fernanda Ester (1997). *Cidade Espetáculo. Política, Planejamento e City Marketing.* Curitiba, Brazil: Editora Palavra.

Samek, Jorge (1996). *A Curitiba do Terceiro Milênio.* Curitiba, Brazil: Editora Palavra.

_____ (1996, 1997). Newspaper articles, *Gazeta do Povo, Espaco Aberto.*

Schwartz, Hugh (1998). *Rationality Gone Awry? Decision Making Inconsistent with Economic and Financial Theory.* Westport, CT and London, England: Praeger (paperback, 2000).

_____ (2003). "The Economic Analysis Underlying Decision Making in Large Corporations (As Revealed in On-Going Interviews)." Presentation to Biennial Meeting, Society for the Advancement of Behavioral Economics. Lake Tahoe, Nevada, July 28-31.

Servicio Brasileiro de Apoio as Micro e Pequenas Empresas (SEBRAE) (n. d. 1997?). *Pesquisa-Piloto de Avaliação/Acompanhamento do Empretec.* Brasilia.

SEBRAE (Servico de Apoyo as Micro e Pequenhas Empresas) and PUC-PR (Pontificia Universidade Católica do Paraná) (1993). *Perfil do Empresário da Pequena Empresa do Paraná.* Curitiba, Brazil.

Slovic, Paul, Melissa Finucane, Ellen Peters and Donald G. MacGregor (2002). "Rational Actors or Rational Fools: Implications of the Affect Heuristic for Behavioral Economics." *Journal of Socio-Economics.* Vol. 31, Issue 4: 329-42.

Stein, Jay M. (1995). *Classic Readings in Urban Planning: An Introduction.* New York: McGraw Hill Publishing Co.

Steiner Neto, Pedro José (1998). *A Percepção dos Resultados Esperados Pelos Beneficiários como Fator de Influência no Processo Decisório.* Ph.D. Dissertation, Department of Administration, University of São Paulo. São Paulo, Brazil.

Temple, Marion (1994). *Regional Economics*. London: St. Martin's Press.

Transurbs (1998). *Guia do Transporte Colectivo de Curitiba*. Curitiba, Brazil: Editora de Guias de Curitiba.

Trindade, E. M. C., D. Oliveira and A. C. A. Santos (1997). *Cidade, homen e natureza*. Uma história das políticas ambientais de Curitiba. Curitiba, Brazil: UniLivre.

Unknown Compiler (October 1999). *Urban Public Transportation Systems Curitiba, Brazil*. Contains articles by Carlos Ceneviva, the former Manager of Curitiba's Bus transit system, Lucas Nieri, a Curitiba architect, and Kenneth E. Kruckemeyer, Research Associate, Center for Transportation Studies, Massachusetts Institute of Technology. The article by Ceneviva is a translation of Ceneviva, n. d. [1999?]

URBS, City of Curitiba [late 1990s]. *Curitiba Integrated Transportation Network: Urban Tranportation World Reference*. Curitiba, Brazil.

U. S. Department of Transportation (2001). *Proceedings of the FTA/ Paraná Bus Rapid Transit Workshop*. Curitiba, Paraná, Brazil. December 10-13,2000.

Wright, Charles L. (1996). "A bus system for the 21st century." *Passenger Terminal World* (Spring): 18-22.

_____ (1998). *The Roles of Buses, Walking, and Cycling in Latin American and Caribbean Cities*. Washington, DC: Inter-American Development Bank:Technical Note RE1-98-005 (March).

_____ (2000). *Modos de Transporte, Utilización del Espacio Urbano y Accidentes de Tránsito*. Washington, D.C.: Inter-American Development Bank: Technical Note RE1-020-F11 (September).

_____, Jennifer L. Cody and Juan Ortega (2000). *Population Density and Urban Transport Planning: Contrasting Cities in the Americas*. Washington, D. C. Inter American Development Bank, Regional Operations Department 1: Technical Note RE1-031-F11-RG (December).

*   *   *

Interviews (Accompanied in the case of most enterprises by annual reports or other company documents). Many persons occupied positions in the public as well as private sectors during their careers; those most identified with official entities or private enterprises at the time of the interviews are listed following the name of that entity unless they were prominently associated with another entity during the course of their careers.

Metropolitan Curitiba Region

Audi: Geraldo Rangel
Argentine Consulate: Jaime Hernando Beserman, Consul; Ricardo José Zuberbuhler, Deputy Consul
Avenida 7. Materiales Hidráulicos: Cesar Luis Gonçalves
Barion & Cia.: Roberto Barion, Industrial Director
Barros, Sérgio Silveira de
Berneck: Gilson Mueller Berneck, President
Boschetti, Ivo Luiz: President, AECIC, Diretor Presidente, Krone
BrasHolanda: Eduilton Ostroski, Administrative Director
BrasilSat: Carlos Henrique de Aragon, Director
Brazilian Institute for Quality and Productivity in Paraná: Adalberto E. Passos, Project Coordinator
Caron, Antoninho
Castro, Demian
Catholic University of Paraná (PUC), Institute of Enterprise Administration: Marcos Mueller Schlemm, Director
Ceneviva, Carlos
CITIPAR: Roberto Camargo
City of Curitiba: Cassio Taniguchi, Mayor; Fabioano Braga Cortes, Chief of Staff; Monica Richbieter, Advisor; Gilberto Luiz Klisiewicz, Director, Department of Planning and Information, Secretary of Industry, Trade and Tourism; Wilhem Meiners, Information Coordinator, Secretariat of Industry, Trade and Tourism; Isac Baril, Director, Financial Administration, Public Supply Center of Paraná
CLAC Dairy Cooperative: Directors, staff
Commercial Association of Paraná: Ardisson Naim Akel, President; Cesar Luiz Gonçalves, Vice President
Construtora Gustavo Berman: Alberto C. Levy
COPEL: Humberto Sanches Netto, Regional Superintendent of Eastern Transmission and other staff
Deconto, Vilson Ronald Riles
Denso do Brasil: Sakuo Noto, Administrative and Financial Director
Electrolux: Luis Carlos Baeta Viera, Director for Special Affairs

Embafort, Indústria Comercial de Artefactos de Madeira: Humberto Ramos Cabral

Equitel: Julio Oscar Fenner Boye, Industrial Director

Fiscinski Dunin, Lubomir (interview in Washington)

FIEP: Jose Carlos Gomes Carvalho, President, Maurilio Schmidt, Chief, Economics Department, Roberto Paredo, Daniel Fedato, economists.

Fontana, João Baptista

Garcia Fernández, Ramón Vicente

Germer, Claus

Hiroshi Yoshizawa, Luiz

Hubner: Nelson Roberto Hubner, Director and Edgar A. Hubner

Industrial City of Curitiba/Development Company of Curitiba: Maria Elisa Ferraz Paciornik, Managing Director, 1995; André Zacharow, President, 1998; Carlos Antonio Scheffel, Sergio Póvoa Pires, Celso Roberto Zem

Indústrias de Madera Zaniolo: Altavir Zaniolo, Director

INEPAR: Renato Requião Munhoz da Rocha, President, Fundacão Inepar

IPARDES: Lourenco, Gilmar M. and Julio Takeshi Suzuki Júnior.

IPPUC: Osvaldo Navaro Alves, President, Mr. Lorival, Economist and Data Coordinator

Jobin Castor, Belmiro Valverde

Kvaerner Pulping: André R. de Ruediger, Administrative and Financial Director

Laboratório Prado: Orley Fedato, Marketing Director

SPVS: Mark Lellovich

Macedo, Mariano de Matos

Magalhães Filho, Francisco

Manuel, Eduardo Guy de

Mari, Mario de

Marques Dias, Eduardo

Mauad, Ulisses

Mendes Lorenso, Gilmar

Oliveira, Dennison de

Passos, Carlos Artur Kruger

Pinheiro, Rubem

Porcile, Gabriel

Prosdócimo, Sérgio

Renault: Carlos Ghosne.

Richbieter, Karlos

Rimi, José: President, SINDEMETAL and Metalúrgica ATRA

Samek, Jorge, City Councilman, Coordinator, Seminar on Curitiba's Master Plan, President, Workers Party of Paraná.

SEBRAE: Helio Cadore, Superintendent, Curitiba; Rosangela Maria Angonese, Director, EMPRETEC.

Siemens: Paulo A. M. Maranhão Faria, Business Development Director

Springer Passos, Adair.

State of Paraná: Elcio Luiz Coltro and Nelson Justus, Secretariat of Industry, Trade and Economic Development; Miguel Salomão, Secretary of State for Planning and General Coordination; Sérgio José Ferreira de Souza, Director General, Secretariat of State for Urban Development

Steiner Neto, Pedro José

SUND EMBA BHS Indústria de Máquinas: Carlos Decker Neto, Industrial Director

Technological Incubator of Curitiba: Gina Gulinel Paladino and Christine Stainsack

TECPAR: Julio Salamão, Technical Advisor; Managers Graca Maria Simões Luz, Ladislau Nelson Zempulski, Rui Akeo Nakamura and Maria Paula A. Yamada.

Transport Travel Tours: Sergio Levy, Director

URBS: Luiz Filla, Manager, Public Transport

Volvo do Brasil: Carlos Morassutti, Director

Other, State of Paraná

ALCOPAR: José Adriano da Silva, Administrative Superintendent

Campo Mourão: Manuel João Garcia Gimenes, Coordinator, AD City Pole

Cavicchiol, José Antonio: Coordinator, FIEP, President, SIVEDAP, Director, Esport Wilson

Hussmann Fast Frio: Jose Antonio Paulatti, President and Armando Melgarejo

Hidro Metalúrgica: Carlos Walter Martins Pedro

Industrial Incubator of Londrina: Director, four small businessmen (brief interviews).

Londrina: Kentaro Takahara, Executive Director, Industrial
Development Plan; Alex Canziani, staff member.
Maringá: Secretary of Industry, Commerce and Tourism: Miguel
Fuentes Sala.
NOMA Truck Maringá: João Noma, President, Carlos Walter
Martins Pedro
Recco Confeccões: Antonio Recco
Volnix: Luiz Donizetti, President.

São Paulo

FIESP: Carlos Alberto R. Orellana, Chief, Economics Department,
Tánia Maria Peres Maitan and other members
State of São Paulo, Secretariat of Commerce and Tourism: Jorge
Eduardo Suplicy Funaro, Chief of Staff
State of São Paulo, Secretariat for Economics and Planning: Luiz
Antonio Diorio
_____, Secretariat for Science and Techology: Emerson Kapaz,
Secretary and Israel Elias.
U. S. Consulate: Gilberto Donahue.
VITAE: Gina G. Gomes Machado.

Index

*For exposition of acronyms, see Glossary and Guide to Acronyms, 135-138.